THE BHS Manual of Equitation

OFFICIAL BHS MANUALS

published by Kenilworth Press

THE BHS Manual of Equitation

The Training of Horse and Rider

The British Horse Society

Consultant Editor: ISLAY AUTY BA, FBHS

KENILWORTH PRESS

This revised edition published in 2001 by
Kenilworth Press Ltd
Addington
Buckingham
MK18 2JR

Reprinted 1994, 1997, 1998, 2001, 2003 and 2005

British Library Cataloguing in Publication Data
A catalogue record for this book is available from the British Library.

ISBN 0-872119-33-6

Layout by Kenilworth Press
Line drawings by Dianne Breeze

Printed in Great Britain by Bell & Bain Ltd, Glasgow

CONTENTS

PREFACE

The British Horse Society's *Manual of Equitation* is based on the classical lines first written about by Xenophon (430-354 BC), maintained by the Spanish Riding School in Vienna and now amended for competitions by the Fédération Equestre Internationale.

Whilst it is difficult, if not impossible, to lay down hard and fast rules on the training of the horse and rider, and horsemastership in general, the *Manual of Equitation* is a consensus of opinion of the national authorities and represents the general view in Britain of equitation and horsemastership. No absolute doctrine has evolved, for Britain is a country where individuality is cherished and different horses, riders and trainers may be suited to different methods. Where, therefore, two methods are practised extensively and successfully in Britain, both are discussed. This book is the result of many eminent members of the British Horse Society devoting a good deal of time voluntarily to discussing and writing about the subject.

The first *Manual of Equitation* was edited by Jane Kidd and Barbara Slane Fleming FBHS. This new edition has been carefully revised and updated by Islay Auty FBHS, and completely re-illustrated by Dianne Breeze.

About this Book

This book is divided into two parts: Training the Rider and Training the Horse. Inevitably, though, the two parts are interlinked, as it is impossible to learn to ride and progress without becoming involved in the way the horse moves, develops, improves and thinks.

Readers are therefore invited to dip into both parts of the book, referring back and forth for specific advice on training, be it for rider or horse, or both. The clear chapter headings and the comprehensive index will allow readers to move around the book easily, finding all the information they need to take their riding and the training of their horse forward to a higher level.

Riders wanting to learn more about related subjects such as saddlery, bitting and specialist care of the competition horse, should refer to the companion volume – *The BHS Complete Manual of Stable Management* – which deals with these matters in some depth.

Training the Rider

CHAPTER

GETTING STARTED

Why learn to ride?

Riding is a unique sport in that it requires not only the participation of a human athlete, but also the active involvement and cooperation of a horse (or pony). It is a sport/activity that can be enjoyed by anyone, from a very early age (three or four years) to active old age. Many riders continue to enjoy their sport for an entire lifetime. Riding can be equally enjoyed individually or as a group activity involving family and/or friends.

Riding is an accessible sport, and while initial introduction may be through a friend or by enrolling at a riding school, the opportunities for developing the interest are huge. Horsemen and women can take part in and specialise in any of the following activities:

- hacking and recreational riding
- endurance or long distance riding
- BHS Trec (combining orienteering skills with basic cross-country riding and requiring accuracy and obedience tests)
- dressage
- show jumping
- eventing
- polo
- showing horses/ponies in hand and under saddle
- racing

While riding is a sport, the level of fitness it requires can be as variable as the intensity of the involvement. For a person who rides for an hour once a week as a recreational rider, the physical fitness required would be relatively low. For a rider taking part in national or international competitions, the need for a high level of mental and physical fitness is as essential as for any other top-level athlete.

Riding is stimulating, challenging, exhilarating, and, above all, fun. The partnership and camaraderie that can develop between horse and human makes this sport quite unique.

Where to start

Initial interest in wanting to learn to ride is often sparked by a connection with someone else who already enjoys the sport. Whether children grow up with horses as part of their life and environment, or whether they become involved through peer pressure or school participation, the initial stimulus can quickly become an all-consuming passion.

Growing up with horses was very common for rural children in Britain before the Second World War, as in those days horses were still actively used in farming and transportation. In the latter half of the twentieth century riding developed into a fashionable pastime. For many children it fell into a similar category to learning a musical instrument, playing football/cricket or dancing – and many adults who had been denied the opportunity to

British Horse Society Examination System

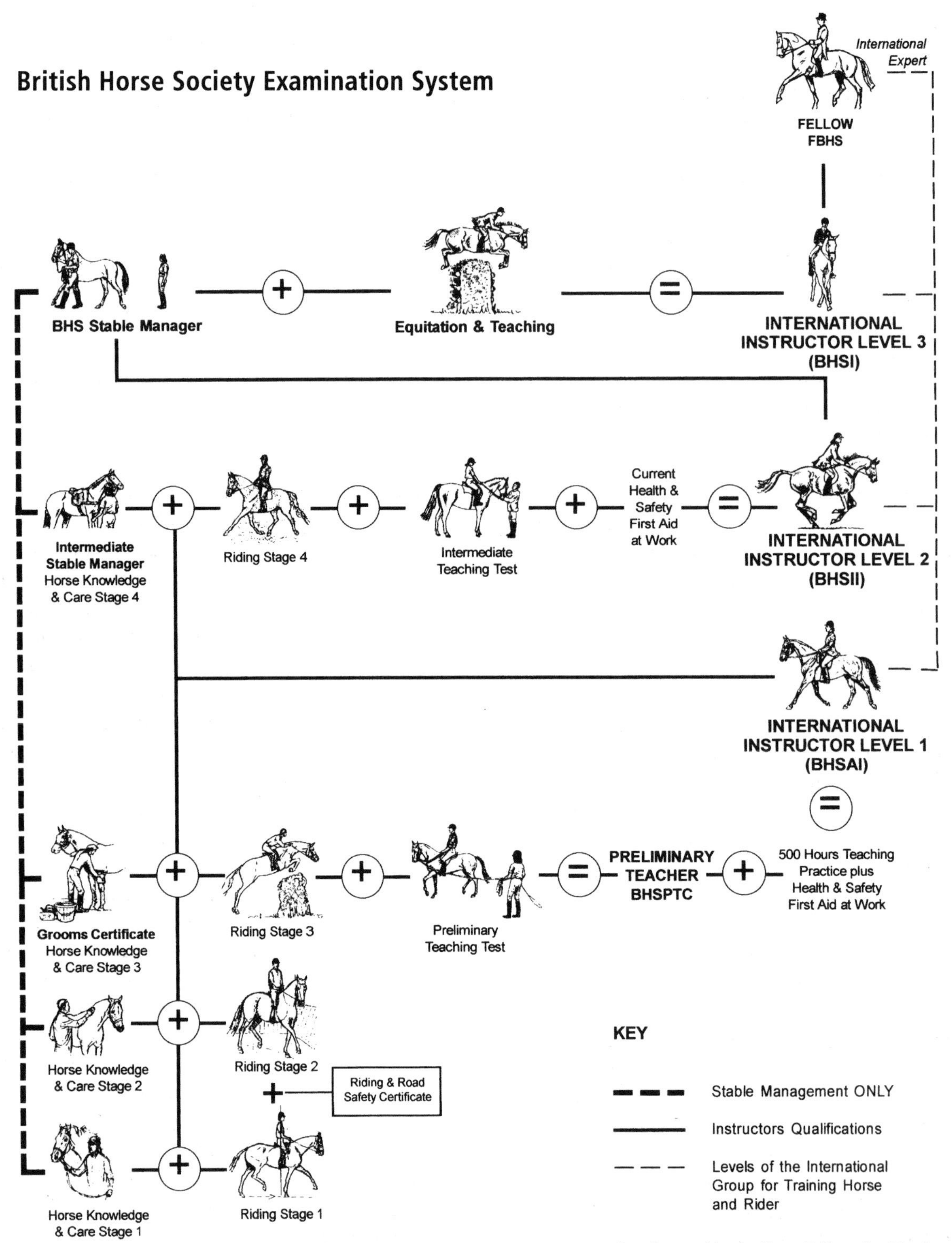

Based on an idea by Karen Tolley – Equi Study

ride in childhood took up the sport with relish in mid-life or even on retiring.

Any sport has its risks. When climbing onto a horse and learning to develop balance and control, there will be the inevitable occasion when one or both are lost and a fall occurs. This is an occupational hazard, but the risks can be minimised by careful choice of where to learn to ride. Being 'taught' by a friend can reduce the worry of working with unfamiliar people and horses, but it lacks the safeguards that choosing a professional riding school will ensure.

Whether choosing a riding school to begin to learn to ride for the first time, to enjoy an hour's hacking or to receive tuition to a more advanced level, it is essential to choose one that is reputable and well run. The British Horse Society (BHS) is the governing body of recreational riding in the UK and it maintains a register of Approved Establishments, which have been inspected to a guaranteed standard. The first requirement for any riding school to operate in the UK is that it holds a Local Authority licence. This indicates that the school has third party insurance cover. The BHS ensures that all its Approved schools hold this licence. Inspection also covers the standard and quality of horses used, the maintenance of facilities, and the qualifications of full- and part-time staff. An Approved riding school will offer advice on correct and safe clothing for riders and will not allow clients to ride without appropriate protective head wear. It will also have at least one qualified instructor holding a BHS teaching qualification. BHS-qualified instructors are required to be members of the Register of Instructors, which ensures that they attend regular updating training at least every two years. They are also required to maintain an up-to-date certificate of first aid by attending either an equine-specific first-aid course or a four-day Health and Safety at Work course, with relevant refresher courses to maintain competence. The BHS publishes a comprehensive book of all its Approved establishments, listed by region nationwide. This can be obtained in all good bookshops or direct from the BHS headquarters at Stoneleigh (see address at the back of the book).

The riding school

Realistically, location is a major factor when first choosing a suitable riding school. Often, however, once a person has some experience of riding, he or she may seek out a school that caters better for his or her individual needs, even if that school is further away or more difficult to get to.

Whether making that first contact by telephone or visiting the school in person, expect a friendly, efficient, professional reception – first impressions count. Being constantly greeted by a telephone-answering machine is not acceptable (except after hours or perhaps at lunch times).

When you visit the yard – which may well be busy – as a potential client the school should make it its business to find time for you. The interest shown to you on that first visit may reflect how you will later be treated as a regular client. You should be escorted around the premises, and shown the facilities and some of the horses. Any questions you have should be clearly answered. Equally, the member of staff showing you round should be making polite enquiries about your aims and requirements. You should be made to feel welcome, relaxed and at ease with the surroundings – so much so that you will come away looking forward to your first lesson.

The facilities offered by riding schools vary widely depending on the size, location and instruction available. A large establishment boasting wonderful facilities may not, in terms of tuition, be any better than a small centre with only a few horses and one proprietor/instructor. A small establishment may show a far greater commitment to good practice, with the bonus of paying individual attention to each client.

It is essential to look beyond the facade of the facilities and assess the atmosphere and commitment level of the centre. What you should be looking for is good, safe, constructive teaching geared wherever possible to the needs and requirements of the individual.

Facilities such as an indoor school, outdoor all-weather surface, show jumps, and cross-country fences, should all be well maintained. Facilities may be old but should not appear neglected. Stable yards should be neat and tidy, and the stable doors should look as if they have seen a coat of paint in the last five years. Broken fencing, weed-infested yards, fields overburdened with docks, thistles or, worse still, ragwort (a weed that is poisionous to horses), give an air of neglect, which is unacceptable. Horses should look cheerful and in good condition (at any time of the year). The school riding surface should neither show a deep furrow round the outside edge nor raised corners, both of which indicate that the school is rarely levelled or harrowed. Staff and instructors should appear neatly turned out and workmanlike, conveying an image in keeping with the professionalism required by the job. A casual attitude around horses ultimately leads to accidents. Tell-tale signs of faulty protocol might include smoking, no clear policy for bringing horses to and from lessons, failing to control the mounting and dismounting groups of riders.

The best way to find a riding school is by recommendation. Even so, you should still visit the school before you book your first lesson, just to be sure that you feel comfortable about all you see.

The instructor

The term 'instructor' possibly has its origins in the military aspect of riding, which has evolved from extensive use of the horse in the cavalry. These days the term can just as easily be synonymous with 'teacher', 'coach' or 'trainer'. While there are minor differences in definition, all refer to a person who imparts knowledge to another, in this instance in the art or sport of riding. The instructor must possess many qualities, perhaps the most valuable one being patience. Motivation is essential, and there must be an ongoing desire to impart knowledge. Understanding and knowledge of the psychology of both horse and rider are other essential attributes, as is being thoroughly conversant with the subject being taught.

Instructors have a responsibility to keep up to date with current thinking and knowledge in the horse world. This in turn enables them to maintain credibility and effectiveness with their pupils. Most riders, certainly at higher levels, will gravitate towards a trainer who can demonstrate his own ability in the sport, or who has a past or present competitive record.

Instructors must be fair, open-minded, honest and good communicators. They must have a high standard of personal integrity and should show a commitment to all their pupils, talented or otherwise. They must be able to develop their own style and philosophy, but must act with professionalism in all circumstances. This should include a personal code of conduct, dress and behaviour, which should uphold the standards of the profession.

An instructor holding a BHS qualification should be proud to be a member of the Register of Instructors. This register benefits both instructor and public alike.

- For the instructor it provides acknowledgment of a commitment to provide good instruction based on achieving a world-renowned professional qualification. It conveys comprehensive insurance and ensures regular updating of methods and information through a range of recognised training courses. It lays down a code of conduct, by which the instructor must abide.
- Members of the public can be confident that they will be taught by a well-trained and acknowledged instructor. Validity of qualifications can be checked. There is reassurance that a registered instructor will provide tuition with due regard for safe practice. The refresher courses that have to be attended mean that the instructor's practice is current. The instructor holds an up-to-date first-aid certificate, has attended a Child Protection course, and is covered by public liability insurance.

It is the instructor's ongoing responsibility as a trainer to assess each rider or group of riders that he/she teaches. This applies as much to clients in a 'one-off' session as to those who are taught regularly. Each lesson must have a plan as a result of the assessment, and the instructor must be able to put the plan into practice, making adjustments as necessary, depending on developments in the session. There should be an aim or goal for each lesson, and it should be achievable. As each session progresses, evaluation must take place. Feedback from the lesson should be positively utilised. Future lesson plans can be based on this.

Clothing

Riding, like many sports, can (though not necessarily) involve its participants in spending large amounts on specialist equipment. As a rider's interest and involvement grow, so too do the opportunities for spending more on clothing etc.

For the new rider the most essential piece of clothing is a riding hat. Some riding schools will hire hats to the public for the first few lessons until interest is assured. It is advisable for the rider to purchase his or her own hat as soon as possible. The hat should have one of the following labels inside it, which ensures that it is of a minimum standard of safety for day-to-day riding and in due course for competition:

PAS 015; ASTM 1163; and EN 1384

It is wise to purchase a hat from a reputable outfitters or saddlery shop, where someone with knowledge of hat fitting can give advice. When buying a hat for a child it is not sensible to buy one that is too big so that it allows room for growth. A well-fitting hat is the number one safety item for riding, which is, after all, a sport with an element of risk. Investment in a correct fit is money well spent.

Correct footwear is the second item where riding safety is concerned. Short jodhpur boots, worn with riding trousers, jodhpurs or jogging bottoms, are ideal. Any type of long riding boot, including economical rubber riding boots, cheaper 'off-the-peg' leather boots, and sophisticated, expensive, made-to- measure boots, is appropriate. These could be worn with breeches. Jodhpurs and breeches are specifically designed for riding and are therefore the most comfortable.

In the early stages stout walking shoes with a small heel (but not with a heavily ridged sole) are good, as are any type of sturdy low-heeled shoes which are secure on the foot and not adorned with protruding buckles or sporting fashionable heels. Trainers are not suitable because of the risk that the unheeled shoe may slip right through the stirrup. Similarly many wellington boots with ridged soles are not easy or very safe to ride in. There are various types of custom-made, inexpensive 'paddock boots' available from many saddlery outlets, and these are fine to start with.

Gloves are advisable, and manufacturers now offer a wide range designed for riders.

With regard to other clothing, the keys words are comfort and safety. Riding is a sporting activity, so clothing should fulfil the following criteria:

- warm in winter: gloves and extra socks may be needed to protect the extremities;
- weatherproof: if riding outside, waterproof clothing may be a must; Goretex clothing provides breathable protection from wet and wind;
- lightweight: several lightweight layers are preferable as these can be shed one by one and are not as restrictive as one bulky layer;
- comfortable: clothing should not be tight, which would limit flexibility and movement.

Avoid fashion clothing – it probably won't be up to the job.

Flowing sleeves, scarves, flapping clothing or dangling jewellery can all be potentially dangerous around horses.

The novice rider's horse

The novice rider's horse must be:

- even tempered and sensible;
- genuinely forward going but with calmness and an unflappable temperament;
- tolerant of variations in aid application, accepting a lack of coordination and often a loss of balance in the rider;

- smooth and fluent in his paces, and moving calmly and evenly through up and down transitions (changes of pace).

The ideal novice rider's horse is worth his weight in gold. In riding schools the type of horse that will generally tolerate the inadequacies of the beginner rider is highly valued indeed.

The ideal horse will often be of half-bred breeding, and his build will not be too fine or lightweight. A middleweight type will usually provide a broader back, on which the novice will feel more secure.

The horse's reactions must be smooth, but he must react nonetheless. After just the first few lessons a very idle horse can prove extremely depressing for a novice. At that stage beginners are starting to learn to use their legs, albeit weakly and sometimes with little effect. This is when the genuine novice rider's horse will respond generously to the often inadequate aid, thus giving the rider encouragement and a sense of achievement. The novice rider then thrives on this success, and his skill and coordination grow as a result.

Novice riders' horses are often by nature kind, both in and out of the stable; they are giving and forgiving. It is essential that their affable nature is not abused unwittingly nor taken advantage of. Interestingly, this type of horse will usually have one 'gear' for riders that he assesses as being nervous or of limited experience, yet when ridden by a more competent rider he will 'move up a gear' and seem to relish the experience of having a better pilot.

In the management of school horses and the maintenance of their morale, it is absolutely essential that the good novice rider's horse is used for a variety of work. Being ridden only by novices will eventually deaden his willingness and depress his generosity and acceptance. Novice riders, through no fault of their own, burden horses with poor coordination and balance. Often their aids are rough, poorly timed or muddled. To maintain the quality of his work and to keep him cheerful the school horse should not become purely a vehicle for the beginner rider.

Inevitably some novice riders will have their first experience of riding on a mount belonging to a friend or relative. Here a few words of caution are needed. School horses are very special animals. They are nurtured and maintained for the qualities outlined above. However genuine a privately owned horse may seem, he will, for the most part, be very familiar with the way he is regularly ridden by his owner. He may not be able to understand or cope with the inadequacies of a novice rider, because he has no experience in this area. Through no fault of his own his reactions to the 'strange' beginner rider could be unpredictable.

The riding arena

Many riding schools possess both indoor and outdoor arenas. As the name suggests, an indoor arena will be enclosed, with a roof, and an outdoor school will be enclosed by some kind of perimeter. Both arenas will have some kind of artificial surface on which the horses work.

Arenas for dressage competition and practice are either 20m x 40m, or 20m x 60m, and most arenas are built to these standard dimensions. Outdoor arenas may be considerably larger, allowing two or more dressage arenas to be set up within the area. Increasingly, premises with these types of facility are used as regular competition venues. With the ever-increasing popularity of dressage as a sport, more and more centres offer all-weather surfaces for both working-in and competing on. These centres are favoured for the higher level of competition, where the well-being of very valuable dressage horses becomes more important. With the increase of winter competitions, again these venues become well utilised, often with monthly shows.

Surfaces range from the more old-fashioned and less used wood-based covering (bark or shavings) through traditional ranges of sand, to the more favoured plastic, rubber or synthetic surface.

To the inexperienced eye, the letter markers around a

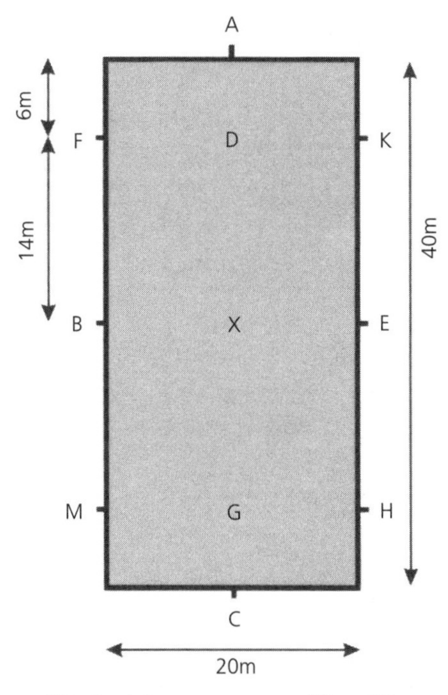

Standard dressage arena – 40m x 20m.

dressage arena seem to follow no clear pattern or system.

In a standard 20m x 40m arena the markers A–F–B–M–C–H–E–K are used, with D, X and G being the 'invisible' markers on the centre line. These markers, with the addition of V–S–R–P–I and L in the larger arenas, are used to enable the rider to follow instructions in the arena. Instructors also use these markers as reference points when teaching riders to execute movements and figures; and in dressage competitions, where riders are required to fulfil a pre-set test, again the markers are used for reference.

Memorising the sequence and position of the markers can be a problem for the beginner rider. The basic set of markers, which will be used in the training of novice riders, can be remembered by the following mnemonic:

A Fat **B**ay **M**are **C**an **H**ardly **E**ver **K**ick

A code of practice/etiquette is observed when riding in arenas, whether indoors or outside:

- Before entering or leaving the arena other riders must

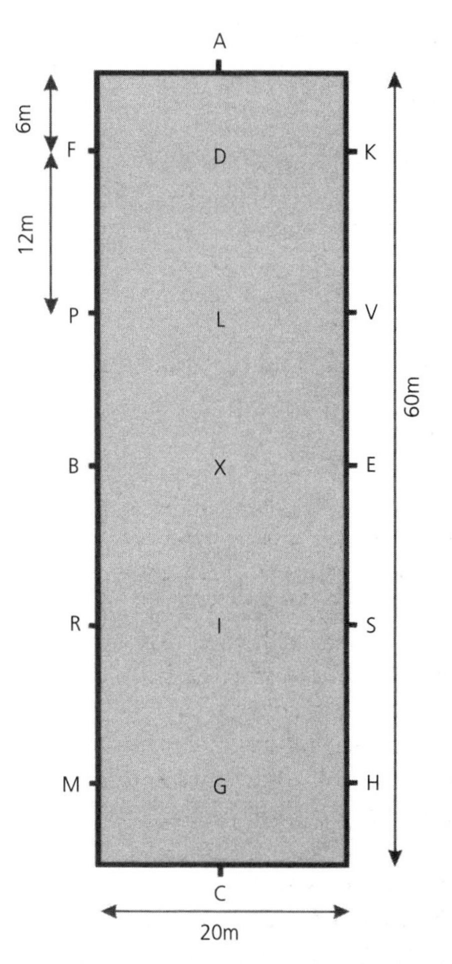

International size dressage arena – 60m x 20m.

be aware of your intent, so that in the interests of safety, a request to open a door or gate is known to all.

- Mounting and dismounting should take place in the centre of the school, away from the track.
- Riders in walk should leave the outer track free for faster gaits.
- Riders should pass left hand to left hand, and riders using lateral work have priority on the track over basic gaits.
- Equipment such as jumps should be stored outside the arena.

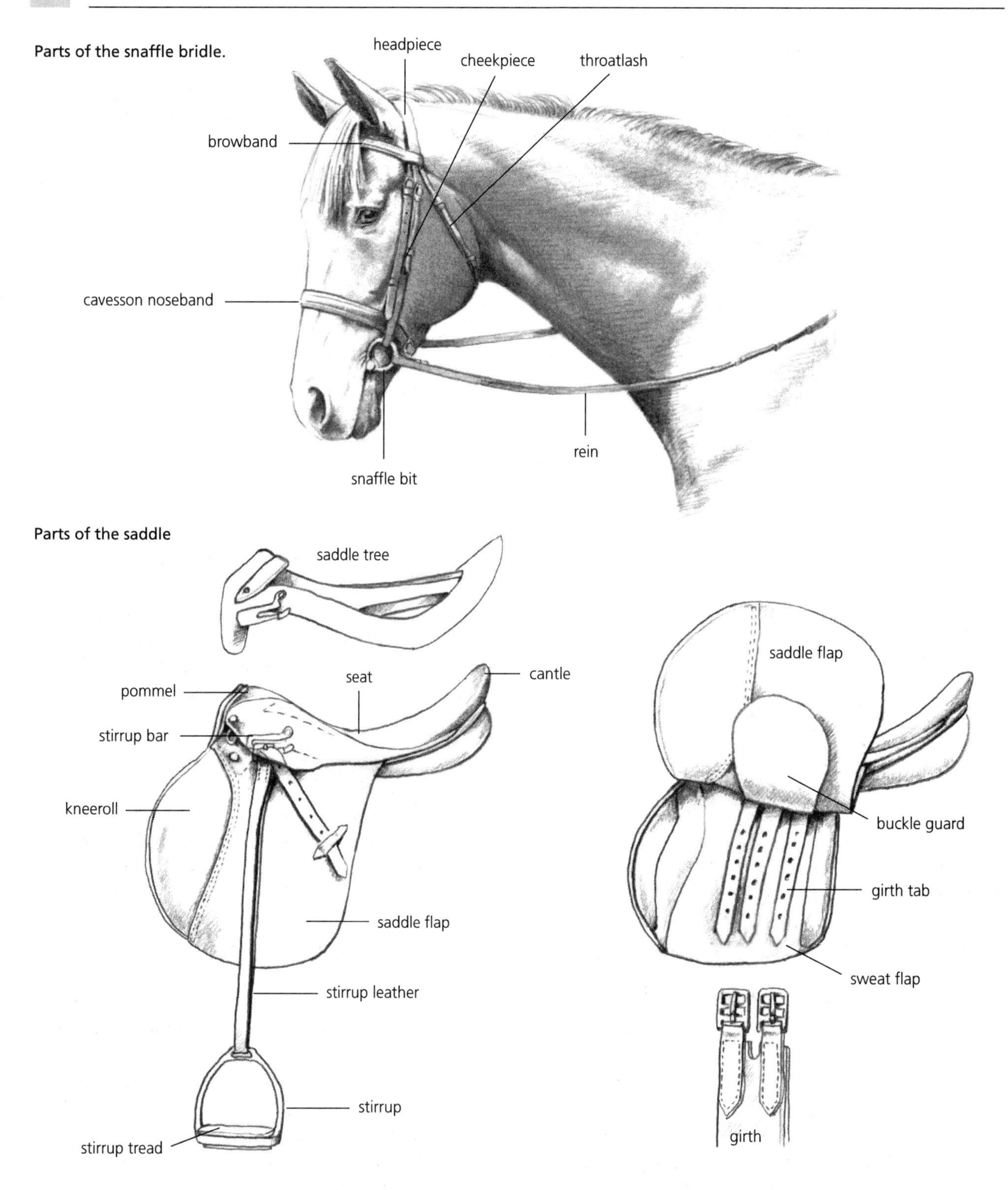
Parts of the snaffle bridle.
headpiece
cheekpiece
throatlash
browband
cavesson noseband
rein
snaffle bit
Parts of the saddle
saddle tree
seat
cantle
pommel
stirrup bar
kneeroll
saddle flap
stirrup leather
stirrup
stirrup tread
saddle flap
buckle guard
girth tab
sweat flap
girth

Tacked up and ready to ride, complete with a neckstrap.

The horse's basic tack

The novice rider should be familiarised with the basic equipment (or tack) that the horse will wear to be ridden. This introduction to saddlery should occur during the first riding lesson.

The novice rider's horse will wear a bridle (usually with a simple snaffle bit with a single pair of reins).

He will wear a saddle (usually a general-purpose saddle) which is appropriate for an inexperienced rider. Usually he will have a numnah (a soft pad) underneath the saddle to aid his comfort.

Often the horse will wear protective 'brushing' boots on his legs. These boots prevent an injury which could otherwise occur if the horse's legs strike into one another. Whether the horse needs one pair or two, will depend on his action.

Horses used by beginners often wear a neck strap. This is a plain leather strap that is fitted around the horse's neck. If the rider should lose balance or feel unsafe he can hold onto the neck strap to give him a feeling of security and to help regain his balance.
As the rider's ability develops he may be introduced to specialist saddles, such as a dressage or jumping saddle. A jumping saddle will greatly enhance the rider's feel, security of position and effect. A dressage saddle will do the same for a dressage rider.

As the novice rider's experience and interest develop he will broaden his knowledge of and familiarity with the huge range of equipment that is available for the horse, whether for day-to-day care, riding or competition.

Leading the horse in hand

Knowing how to lead a horse is one of the most basic requirements for anyone who is going to ride. Learning to lead the horse should come very early in the education of the novice rider, but to begin with assistance should be given. Most riding schools encourage pupils to lead their horses from the yard or stable to the riding arena.

If leading a number of horses in a line (as in taking a group of horses out to a lesson), it is essential that each leader keeps a safe distance (about half a horse's length) from the horse in front. To be safe, each leader must be aware of what is happening in front and be ready to halt his horse or close up by increasing the pace as necessary.

When lining up a row of horses side by side ready to be mounted, it is essential to maintain a safe distance

The correct way to lead a horse.

between the horses so that there is no risk of kicking or biting and possible injury to horses or riders.

The following description for leading in hand applies to a horse in a snaffle bridle:

- The bridle should be well fitted.
- The reins should be taken over the horse's head.
- The leader takes the reins in both hands, with his right hand close to the bit, and his left hand holding the remainder of the reins towards the buckled end.
- The leader should be in the vicinity of the horse's shoulder or neck, with the horse willingly stepping up alongside him.
- If necessary a whip can be carried in the leader's left hand, to be used if the horse is lazy, with a short, sharp reminder on the left flank.
- The leader should march briskly (or run if in trot), staying close to the horse, but allowing the horse to move freely without restriction by the reins.
- The leader should command the horse to 'Walk on', or to 'Whoa' or 'Ter-rot' as required.
- A purposeful, confident manner will instil confidence and obedience in the horse.
- Authority in voice and body language will instigate submission from most horses.

Horses can be led in a headcollar or halter provided that the horse is calm, obedient, well trained and in an off-road situation (e.g. from field to stable, or from stable to riding arena).

Mounting and dismounting

These basic and most essential skills are often superficially covered in basic riding tuition. Neglect of safe and effective procedures for mounting and dismounting can easily lead to an unnecessary accident or damage to the horse, rider and saddle.

Control of the horse while mounting is a must. For the novice rider, the horse should be held to ensure that he stands still. A clear demonstration should be given to the beginner so that the correct procedure has been

Mounting from the ground.

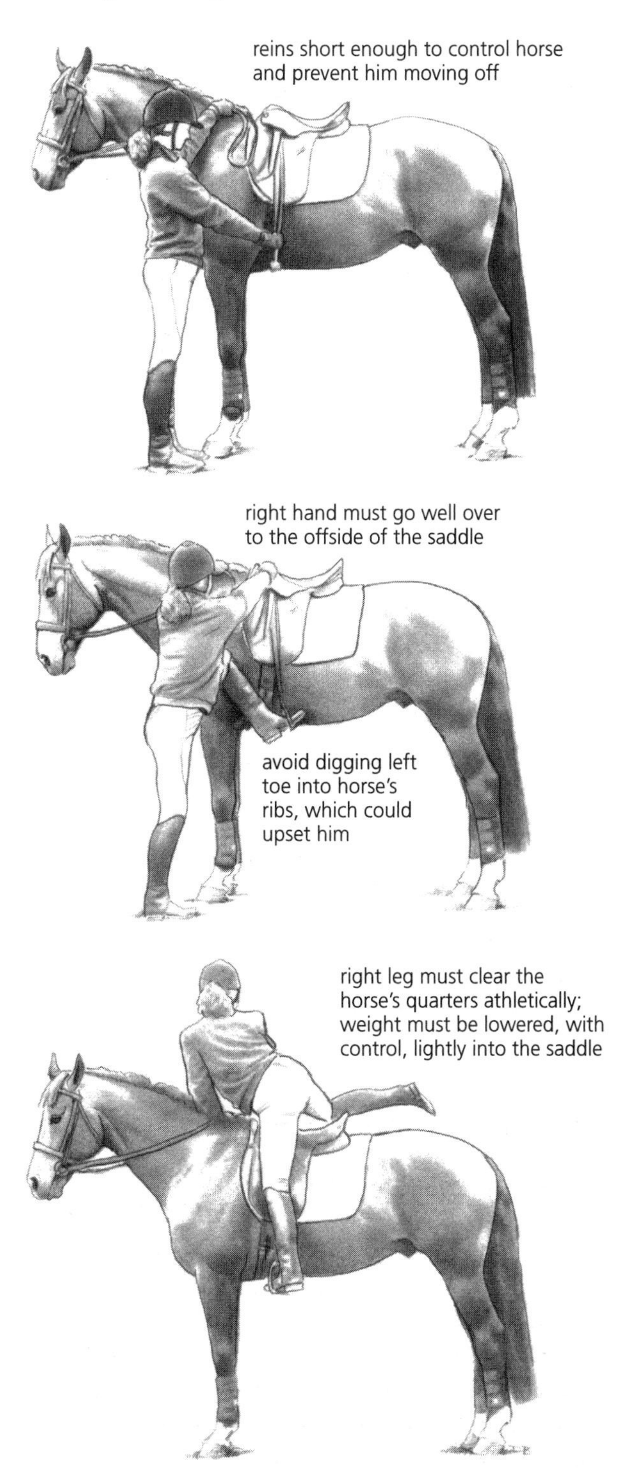

observed before mounting is attempted. Even though the horse may be held by an assistant, the rider must always take responsibility for gathering up the reins – if not, there may be an occasion when the horse is not being held, the rider does not pick up the reins (through lack of habit) and the horse moves during mounting, which could cause an avoidable accident.

The mounting procedure can be broken down into the following elements.

- Make sure that the girth is firm, that the stirrups are run down, and that the reins have been taken over the horse's head onto his neck.
- Pick up both reins in the left hand (and a chunk of mane to help security); at the same time turn to face the horse's tail.
- Take the near-side stirrup in the right hand and place the left foot into it (avoid putting the toe into the horse's side).
- With two or three energetic springs, bounce off the ground and simultaneously place the right hand over the saddle and hold the skirt of the saddle on the far side. If the rider is short, he may find it easier to place the right hand on the pommel or just the far side of it.
- Mounting should be achieved by pressure on the left stirrup coordinated with a spring up to saddle height. As you spring, swing the right leg well over the saddle cantle and the horse's hindquarters.
- The rider's weight should be lowered into the saddle with control, while the right foot locates the offside stirrup. For the beginner/novice rider assistance will be given on how to take the offside stirrup correctly.
- The reins are then adjusted into both hands.

It is very important that a degree of agility and athleticism is developed – the rider must never pull himself up onto the horse, or bang the horse's quarters through springing with insufficient energy, or land heavily in the saddle.

This mounting procedure should become so securely ingrained in the rider's memory that correct repetition becomes automatic. Poor mounting can precipitate an accident, which could have serious consequences. Poor mounting technique can also subject the rider or horse to back injury; in addition it can, through repetition, damage the saddle, which in turn could cause injury or discomfort to the horse.

It is perfectly acceptable to carry out the described mounting procedure from a mounting block, or from an improvised raised area, such as a step, the bottom of a lorry ramp or a sturdy stool. In all these cases the effort of mounting from the ground is lessened with benefits to the horse, rider and saddle.

Another method of mounting a horse involves being given a 'leg up' from the ground by a competent person. It is useful to watch someone else being given a 'leg up' before receiving one for the first time. There is a certain knack to the process – i.e. the two people involved need to coordinate their actions. Instructions must be clear.

Giving a 'leg up'

The person giving the 'leg up' (usually your instructor) stands close to the horse's near-side shoulder, often with one hand on the bridle to keep the horse still. If not holding the horse, the assistant will use both hands for the 'leg up'.

The rider's left leg is lightly supported at the top of the shin, just below the knee. On the count of three or with just a slight spring from the rider, the assistant pushes the rider into the air. The lift is achieved by the rider's spring, as with the traditional method of mounting. Coordination between the rider and the assistant puts the rider cleanly into the air, and the rider then swings his right leg over the horse's hindquarters and lowers his weight into the saddle gently and with control.

This method of mounting is used throughout the racing industry where racing saddles and ultra-short stirrups prevent mounting from the ground in the usual way. More often than not, young horses are taught to accept the rider being legged up before they learn to cope with the rider mounting from the stirrup. Short people and children often benefit from a 'leg up'.

Receiving a 'leg up'

Unless otherwise instructed the rider should be in control of the horse to prevent him from moving. The reins (and whip if carried) should be in the left hand. (Make sure that the whip cannot interfere with the person giving the 'leg up' – it can safely be held on the offside of the neck.) The rider stands close to the horse, facing the saddle, with the left hand on the pommel and the right hand on the cantle. The left leg is bent at the knee. On the count of three, or as the rider springs into the air, a supporting push under the knee is given from the person on the ground. The right hand is released and the rider lowers his weight gently into the saddle, taking up both stirrups and adjusting the reins into both hands.

Dismounting

To dismount, the horse (under most usual circumstances) should be required to stand still. The rider takes both reins into the left hand (and the whip, if carried) and releases both feet from the stirrups. With a fluent coordinating swing of the upper body forward and the right leg back and up, the rider swings his leg clear of the saddle and hindquarters, and with a bent knee lands lightly by the horse's side.

Dismounting well requires agility and some athleticism. At no time must the horse be inconvenienced by poor dismounting technique.

As the rider lands he should then move to the horse's head to control the horse. Usually after dismounting the stirrups are run safely up the leathers, the girth is slackened and the reins are taken over the horse's head for safe leading.

Traditionally mounting and dismounting are carried out on the horse's left side, but it is good practice and beneficial for horse and rider if the rider becomes competent on both sides.

CHAPTER 2 THE RIDER'S POSITION, AND EARLY LESSONS

Why is position so important?

The basis of all equitation is the ability of the rider to sit in the saddle in the correct classical position and to be able to maintain this position with minimum tension under all circumstances.

The word 'classical' is not used in a pedantic way but refers to a position which has become classical because it has evolved through the ages as the most practical way of riding a horse. Xenophon (430 to 354 BC) wrote of it; it is taught by the Spanish Riding School; and, subject to the certain modifications adopted by the Fédération Equestre Internationale, FEI, it is the basis of this book.

The aim is that a rider should place as much of his weight as possible where the horse can most easily carry it: that is, just behind the withers, near to the animal's centre of balance (also its centre of gravity). By using an upright position the rider can remain in balance with the horse and this is essential if horse and rider are to work together in harmony. Any deviation from this ideal position will be reflected in the horse's way of going and/or his temperament.

It is, therefore, essential that every serious horseman works to achieve a truly classical seat until such a position becomes instinctive for working the horse on the flat.

The above applies also to the classical jumping position, which is achieved by closing the angles of hip, knee and ankle joints, while remaining in balance with the horse.

THE RIDER'S BASIC POSITION

The position described in detail in the following paragraphs is that to be adopted for riding on the flat. As well as being the one from which a rider can most easily influence his horse, it is also the most elegant. The rider sits square in the lowest part of the saddle, his weight equally distributed on his seat bones and absorbed by the seat, thighs and feet, the latter resting on the stirrups with only enough weight to keep the stirrups in place. The rider's point of balance is close to that of the horse: i.e. behind the horse's withers. There must be a minimum of tension, physical or mental, if the correct position is to be achieved and maintained. The muscles should have 'tone' – firmness which lies between extreme relaxation and tension.

Outline from the side

Viewed from the side, the correct outline is shown on the next page, with a vertical line running through the rider's ear, shoulder, hip and heel. This line remains unchanged except in the rising trot. The position of the body viewed from the side should be:

- **Head**. The rider looks in the direction in which he is going, but if he needs to look down, he does so with the eyes only. The head should not be dropped nor poked forward, and the jaw should not be stiff.
- **Shoulders**. Should be down and well back without

The correct position for the rider, as seen from the side. Notice the shoulder-hip-heel alignment.

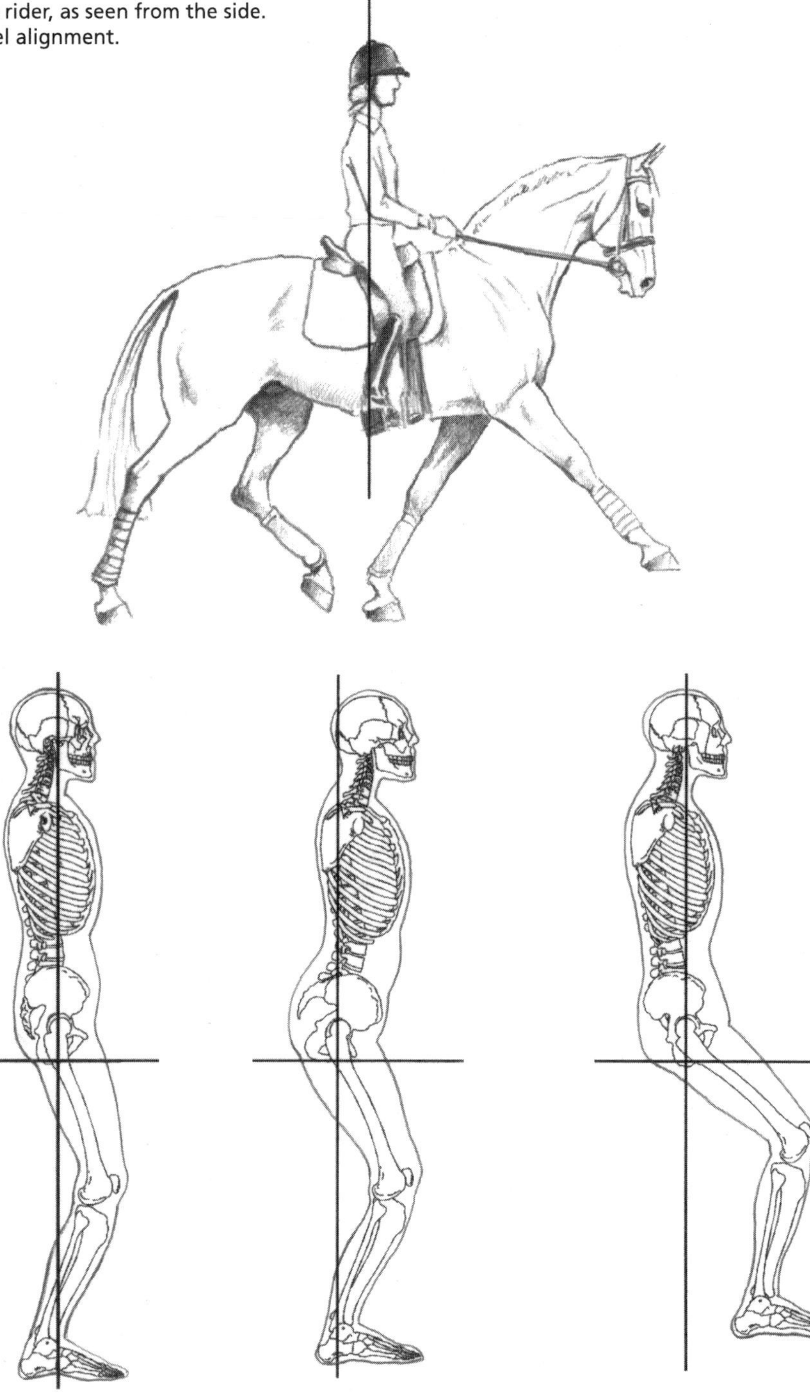

The correct basic position.

Hollow back.

Collapsed seat.

The position of the rider's hands and arms, as seen from the side. When correct, there should be an imaginary line running from the elbow, through the wrist, to the horse's mouth.

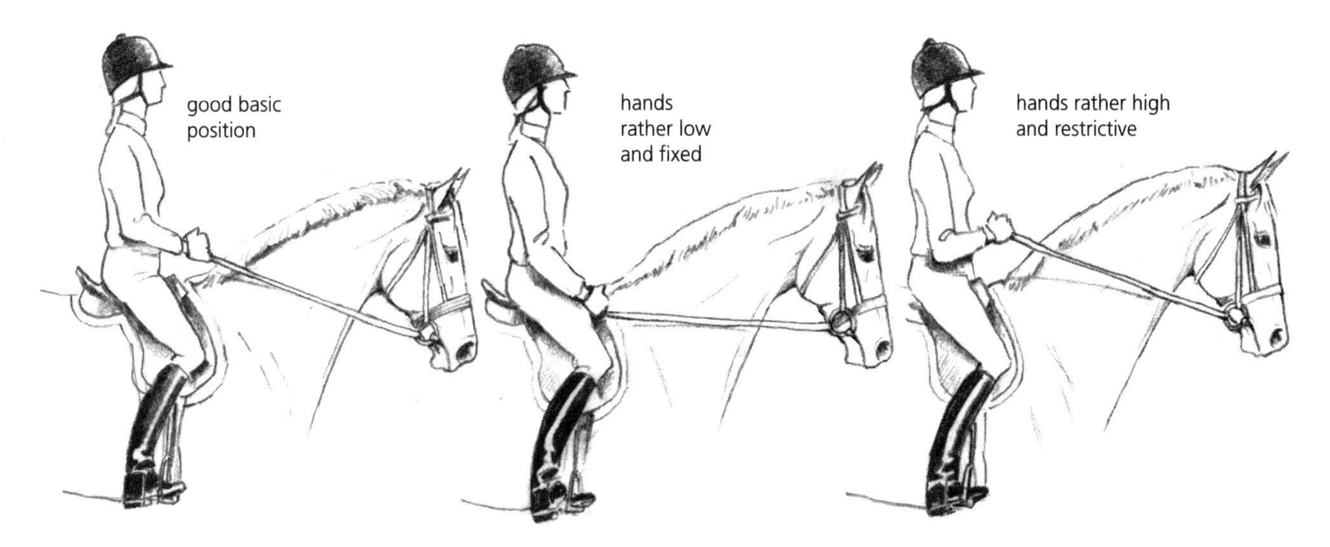

being stiff. This is achieved by expanding the chest rather than squaring the shoulders.

- **Back**. The body is upright, as shown above, with the back straight but supple. It must not be hollowed or collapsed except to the extent that it follows the natural curvature of the spine.
- **Waist**. Should not be allowed to collapse backwards (collapsed seat), forwards (hollow seat), or to one side (collapsed hip.)
- **Hip joints**. These should be pressed slightly forward, with the pelvis upright so that the side seams of the breeches are upright and at right angles to the horse's back.
- **Legs**. The thighs should be flat on the saddle. The muscles should have minimal tone and tension in the thigh, hip joint, or anywhere in the leg. The knee points to the front, as does the toe, helping the rider to sit deeper in the saddle. The knee joint should not be forced into the saddle but should be relaxed so that the lower leg hangs down, lying softly on the horse's side. The legs should have the tone to maintain a constant contact with the horse's sides.
- **Feet**. The widest part of the foot rests on the stirrup iron with only sufficient weight to retain the irons. The stirrup irons should be level, with no extra weight on the inside or outside of the foot, the heel slightly lower than the toe with the ankle joint remaining supple.
- **Arms and hands**. The upper arm should be relaxed, hanging down and not behind the vertical. The shoulders and elbow joints should be flexible to allow the hands to follow the movements of the horse's head. There should be a minimum of tension in the forearm and in the hand and there should be a straight line from the elbow, through the hands to the horse's mouth. Looking from above, the straight line will run from the outside of the forearm, through the back of the hand, down the rein, to the horse's mouth. The thumb should be uppermost. The reins are held at the base of the fingers and come out over the top of the hand, where the thumb rests lightly on them (see also page 53). The fingers should be closed but not clenched, so that if the rider were holding a bird in each hand, the bird would be allowed to breathe but not to fly away.

The rider's position viewed from the rear.

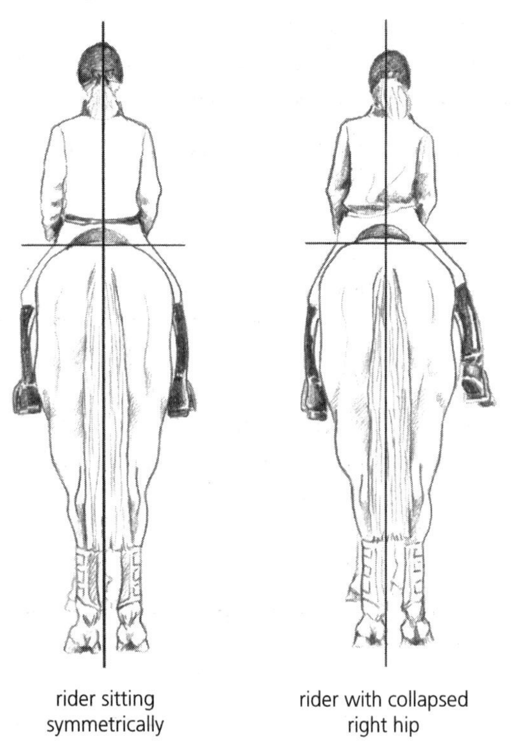

rider sitting symmetrically — rider with collapsed right hip

Outline from the rear

Viewed from the rear (see above) a straight line would run through the middle of the rider's head, down the spine, through the centre of the back of the saddle and the horse's spine. On turns and circles the angle of the rider's body should stay exactly in line with the angle of the horse's body in relation to the ground: i.e. suppleness should allow the rider to move with the horse's movement and follow his direction (see right).

- **Head**. The head and neck must be square on the shoulders and not tilted to either side.
- **Shoulders**. The shoulders should be at equal height without hunching or stiffness.
- **Elbows**. The elbows should be level with one another, not stretched away from the body nor glued to the sides, and should hang naturally.
- **Seat**. The hip joints should be square to the front, with the weight resting evenly on both seat bones, the central seam of the breeches being in line with the centre of the saddle.
- **Lower legs**. The lower legs should be level with one another. They should hang down, not stretched from the horse's sides and with the inside of the lower legs quietly in contact with the horse's sides.
- **Feet**. The feet should be level, and should have equal weight on both stirrup irons without having more weight on the inside or outside of the irons. The ankles should be at equal angles.

The seat

To use the seat correctly when riding it helps to understand its anatomy and methods of movement. At the upper ends of the thighs (femurs) are the balls of the ball-and-sockets of the hip* joints. The sockets of the right and left hip joints are about one third the

Position of horse and rider viewed from above.

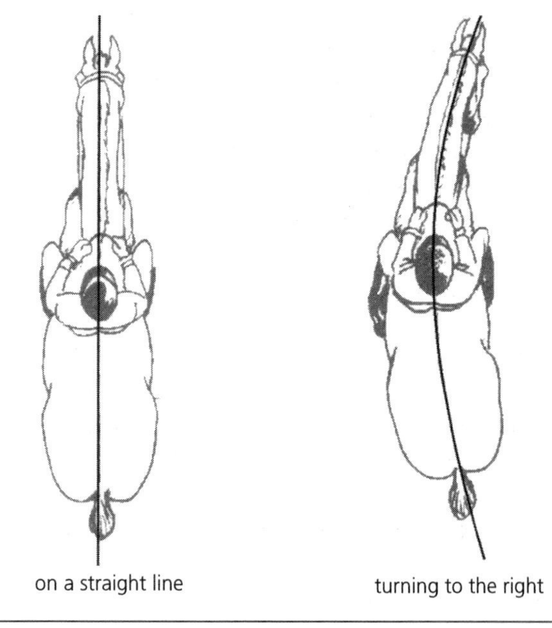

on a straight line — turning to the right

* The term 'hip' tends to be used loosely and may refer to the hip joints or the hip bones, or the iliac crests, or the medical definition of the ischium, ilium and pubis. In this book, to avoid confusion, the medical definition for the hips is used.

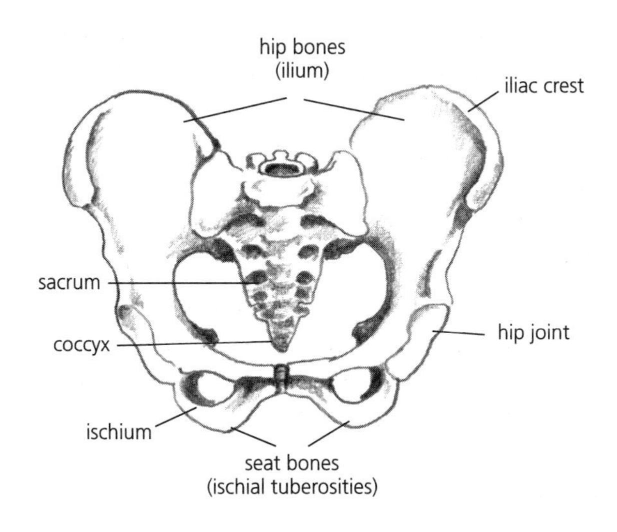

The pelvic girdle.

way up the right and left hip bones (each hip bone consists of the ilium above, the ischium below and behind, and the pubis below and in front – see above). The two hip bones form the front, sides and part of the back of the pelvis which is an oval-shaped (in horizontal section), almost rigid girdle. The lowest points of the pelvis are the seat bones. The ridges of bone at the front of the pelvis which can be felt just below the waist are the iliac crests. The lower forward points of the pelvis which can be felt at the bottom of the abdomen are right and left pubic bones. At the back, the ring of the pelvic girdle is completed by the sacrum. This consists of fused rigid vertebrae which articulate with the lumbar vertebrae which run from just above to just below the waist. They are mobile, and above them the thoracic vertebrae are more rigid. On either side of the lumbar vertebrae are the loins which are the sections of the body on both sides of the spine lying between the hip bones and the false ribs. These are the ribs that are not attached to the breastbone.

The rider can move his seat because:

- The lumbar spine is mobile.
- The pelvis can be tipped. From the pivot of where the rigid sacrum (rear section of the pelvis) and the mobile lumbar vertebrae are connected the pelvis can be tipped forwards (iliac crests forward, pubic bones backward), and backwards, largely through use of the abdominal and back muscles.
- The hip joints enable the thighs and seat to move independently of each other.

The pelvis can also be:

- Tipped sideways (by bending the lumbar vertebrae) when one hip joint is lowered and moves sideways to result in a collapsed hip.
- Turned so that in relation to the trunk this will result in one seat bone moving forward and round and the other backward in the opposite direction.

WHAT TO EXPECT IN THE FIRST FEW LESSONS

Having chosen a riding school and felt confident about the initial contact you made with the centre, you should have been advised about what to wear for your first lesson and whether or not a hat can be hired from the school. On arrival, there should be a clear procedure: either you will be met by your instructor, or you will present yourself to the reception or office, and/or you will study the daily programme to see who will be teaching you and which horse you will be riding. The first few lessons should follow a standard format. The novice rider should be encouraged to handle the horse, and learn to lead it in hand to wherever the lesson will take place. He should be taught how to check the girth, how to run down the stirrups, and how to put the reins over the horse's head. All these activities should be closely monitored and assistance readily offered by the instructor.

Instruction may be in a small group of riders (two to four) of the same standard, or it may be on a one-to-one basis. Private lessons obviously cost more than group lessons.

Beginner riders may be led by a junior member of

Tightening the girth whilst in the saddle.

staff, with one instructor in charge of the actual teaching. Riders may learn on a lead rein or on the lunge – the differences are discussed in greater detail later in the book.

The first few lessons should cover the correct method for preparing to mount the horse, mounting, and of course, dismounting. The basic riding position will be demonstrated, and the rider will be encouraged to try to adopt this at halt before experiencing any movement of the horse.

Picking up the reins, learning how to hold them and how to lengthen and shorten them should be an essential part of the first lesson. Often, however, there will be times in the early sessions when the rider is asked to hold the pommel of the saddle or a neck strap to help balance and security. Riders will also be shown how to tighten the girth and adjust the stirrups from the saddle.

The rider's first experience of horse movement should be in walk, and the rider should be introduced to the concept of transitions up and down, with the accompanying information on the use and coordination of legs and hands to give aids, or messages, to the horse. If the rider is confident and showing no signs of worry or nervousness trot will usually be tried in the first or second lesson.

The duration of lessons for novice riders will usually be thirty or forty minutes maximum. Fitness and ability to concentrate must be the governing factors here,

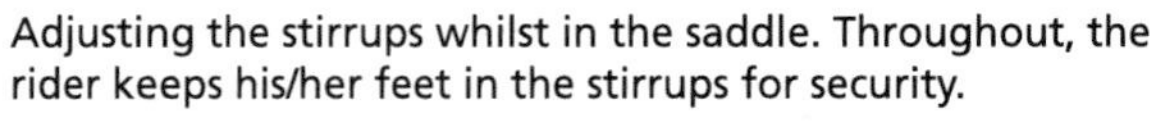

Adjusting the stirrups whilst in the saddle. Throughout, the rider keeps his/her feet in the stirrups for security.

especially at first.

The beginner rider should endeavour to ride at least once a week so that continuity is achieved through reasonably frequent repetition. However, progress will depend on many factors in addition to lesson frequency. Enjoyment and satisfaction must be paramount as well as an overall sense of achievement. This does not mean that every session will result in a burgeoning feeling of success. The general feeling over several lessons, however, must be one of pleasure and progress, even if some of the components of the sessions are difficult or challenging for the rider.

MAKING PROGRESS

So, during the first half dozen lessons the beginner rider can expect to cover the following basic riding skills:

- mounting and dismounting
- the basic riding position
- picking up the reins and holding them
- shortening and lengthening the reins
- the aids for moving forward to walk from halt and from walk to halt

RIDING SCHOOL TERMS

Leading in hand – lead your horse, usually to the area where you will ride and/or back to his stable.

Run down the stirrups – to pull the stirrup irons down the stirrup leathers, ready for use.

Run up the stirrups – to slide the stirrup irons up to the top of the leathers so that they are safe when leading the horse.

'Go large' – ride around the perimeter of the arena/school using the outside track.

'On the right rein' – moving in a clockwise direction.

'On the left rein' – moving in an anti-clockwise direction.

'Change the rein' – make a change of direction from the left rein to the right rein, or vice versa, within the school.

'Inner track' – the inside track, about 1.5m/5ft inside the outer track; usually regarded as allowing room for one horse to pass comfortably on the outside track.

'Pass left to left' – when riding in a school or arena riders traditionally pass left shoulder (or hand) to left shoulder (hand), unless otherwise instructed.

'Take the reins over the head' – both reins are taken over the horse's head, usually to enable the (unmounted) rider to lead the horse in hand.

'Quarter markers' – the arena letters F, H, K and M.

'Half markers' – the arena letters B and E.

'Centre line' – an imaginary line between A and C, the centre of which is X.

'Leading file' – the rider at the front of a line of (single file) riders.

'Rear file' – the rider at the back of a line of (single file) riders.

'Whole ride ...' – means all the riders together.

'In succession ...' – means one rider at a time.

'Prepare to ...' – a term that informs the rider of the need to get ready to give an aid or sequence of aids to tell the horse what to do next.

'Track left' – turn left on reaching the track.

'Track right' – turn right on reaching the track.

'Make much of your horse/pony' – give your horse/pony a pat as a reward.

- the concept of transitions from one gait to another
- how to turn the horse left and right
- developing the walk pace into trot
- the difference between rising and sitting trot
- establishing rhythm and coordination in rising trot
- developing balance and coordination in walk and trot
- basic school figures and terms relating to 'going large' around the school
- riding turns, inclines and circles
- understanding the need to work evenly on both reins
- making changes of rein
- appreciating the value of working without stirrups and gradually developing this work
- working with increasing independence from the leader or lunger
- taking greater responsibility, as balance improves, for controlling the horse
- establishing a more independent riding position

The ability to control the horse (in a novice lesson) without assistance from the ground **may** be achieved in six lessons, but for some riders it may take longer.

The **most import criteria** in these early lessons are that:

- the lessons are enjoyable and constructive;
- the tuition is clear and the rider feels confident to question anything he is unsure about;
- the rider feels positive and enthusiastic to try again after the lesson;
- the horse is never inconvenienced by the efforts of the novice rider;
- the rider should become aware that riding is a partnership and he should be encouraged to communicate with the horse, treating it with respect and not as an inanimate object.

POSITION IN MOVEMENT IN WALK AND TROT

Walk

The horse walks in four time. The walk is a marching gait in which each of the feet is put down individually, one after the other, with no moment of suspension (i.e. when all four feet are off the ground).

He nods his head as each foreleg comes to the ground, and to keep the correct rein contact the rider's hands must invite this movement and not restrict it. The fingers remain closed on the reins and the correct contact is maintained. The rider remains sitting upright, but his supple seat moves to allow and not to restrict the horse's body movements. When the horse walks well there is considerable movement of his back muscles. This movement is essential if the horse is to remain supple, coordinated and free in his gaits. Therefore the rider must allow this movement to occur through supple action of his loins, but not his upper back. It is usual for the pelvis to move in the rhythm of the gait. A good exercise for developing both suppleness and feel is to allow the seat bones to move alternately so that as the left hind leg is lifted forward the rider allows his left seat bone forward in accordance with the horse's muscle movement and then the right seat bone with the right hind leg. This movement in the rider's seat and loins should not be exaggerated and should be barely perceptible to an onlooker.

Trot

The horse trots in two time. His legs move in diagonal pairs: near fore and off hind, off fore and near hind. The trot can be ridden sitting or rising.

Sitting trot

The rider sits softly, with his seat in contact with the saddle. The body remains upright. The movement of the horse's back is absorbed mostly through the rider's loins but also through the seat, thighs, knees and ankles. The hands keep a consistent, elastic contact. The spring of the trot is such that in absorbing the movement, the rider should feel rather as though he is riding the crests of small waves. Thus, the thighs feel supple and the pelvis is cushioned by the seat. As in the walk, the rider's movement must not be exaggerated, resulting in the back hollowing or the waist collapsing. Any excess tension or gripping will cause the rider to bump instead of remaining in a quiet, balanced position in contact with the saddle on the horse's back.

Rising trot

Working in time with the diagonal two-beat trot, the rider rises on one beat of the trot and sits on the next beat. It is essential that this is done in perfect balance so as not to upset the horse's rhythm. The rider's body is inclined slightly forward from the pelvis with the pelvis tipped forward, and he should sit softly without allowing the weight to go backwards. The shoulders and elbows allow the hands to go with the movement of the horse's head and neck, which in the trot hardly move.

Rising trot on a named diagonal

Learning to ride on a particular diagonal is achieved gradually. It is helpful at first to watch the horse's shoulders moving backwards and forwards in the walk. The rider needs to be able to glance down at the shoulder whilst riding the horse forward in the usual way. As the shoulder moves forward, the front foot is off the ground, and as the shoulder moves back towards you, the front foot is taking weight on the ground. Watching in walk will give you the idea of what to look for in trot, when the shoulder action is that much quicker.

To attempt this in trot, start off in sitting trot, as you have been taught, and then establish rising trot. When the trot is forward and in a good rhythm, and only then, start to glance at the shoulders (each one in turn). Try to decide which shoulder is coming towards you as you

Rising on the correct (in this case, left) diagonal.

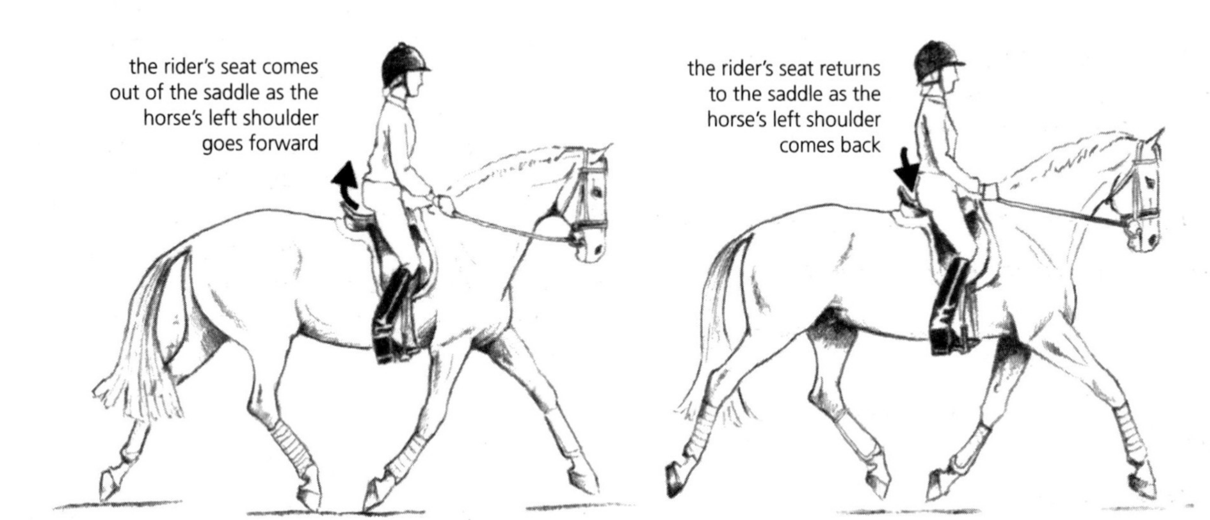

sit in the saddle. If the right shoulder is coming back as you sit, then you are sitting as the diagonal pair of right fore foot and left hind foot meet the ground (this is called the right diagonal – named from the front leg). If you are sitting as the left shoulder is moving back towards you, the left front foot is on the ground and you are on the left diagonal.

Gradually you will become more adept at recognising which diagonal you are on and can then try changing from one diagonal to the other. This is achieved by sitting for an extra beat or 'bounce' in the saddle, which causes you to 'come up' on the other diagonal. Learning to sit for an extra beat takes practice. Changing diagonal in rising trot enables you to ride the horse in good balance and prevents the horse from becoming 'one-sided' as a result of you always sitting on the same diagonal. It also improves your coordination and will, in time, enable you to develop 'feel' as a rider.

LEARNING TO RIDE ON THE LUNGE OR LEAD REIN

There are advantages and disadvantages in both of these very viable means of teaching the beginner rider. Each will be considered on its merits. Ultimately the rider must decide which method he prefers, assuming that both are on offer, and then discuss the issues with the riding school.

Learning on the lunge

- The horse must be safe and experienced as a lunge horse for beginners. He must be calm and obedient.
- The horse's trot should be neither too big nor bouncy, which a novice rider would find difficult to cope with or sit to.
- The instructor must be competent in lungeing the horse well and teaching the novice simultaneously. This arguably requires greater skill than giving a lead-rein lesson.
- The physical demands made on a lunge horse are greater than those made on a lead-rein horse.
- Lungeing requires a one-instructor-to-one-pupil ratio, so is labour intensive.
- Lungeing requires a minimum area of 20m x 20m for the lesson. It is advisable for the area to be enclosed, and with sound footing.
- One horse should not be expected to repeat several lunge lessons daily, nor be lunged on every working day because of the physical effort involved.
- Some novice riders feel insecure when on the end of a lunge rein, well away from the instructor's direct control.
- Some novice riders prefer the greater feeling of independence that the lunge gives them over the lead rein.
- There are limitations in the visibility that the lunger/teacher has of his pupil. Some faults in straightness or position of the outside of the rider may go unnoticed.
- Lungeing can be valuable for developing the position, effect and feel of any level of rider, from novice to advanced.

Learning on a lead rein

- Often more suitable for children and ponies, a number of riders can be taught by one instructor while being led by competent leaders.
- The horse or pony can cope with a number of sessions in one day as leading is far less physically intensive than being lunged.
- Some nervous riders feel more secure and confident in having someone in control of the horse close by.
- In groups, novice riders often gain support and encouragement from each other.
- Some adult riders feel rather belittled by being led.

- The pony/horse must be calm, good tempered, easy to lead in walk and trot on both reins, and comfortable.
- Some beginners may be offered one or two lessons on the lead rein before progressing to the lunge.

After the initial lunge or lead rein lessons the beginner rider should progress to riding unattended when:

- He has basic balance and coordination in walk and trot, independent of the reins.
- He has a basic understanding of the aids to stop, start and turn.
- He is deemed able to develop his skills behind a competent leading file.

CHAPTER

IMPROVING ON THE LUNGE

One of the best ways of establishing the correct position in the saddle and improving a rider's balance is for him to ride without stirrups both on and off the lunge. The main advantage of riding on the lunge is that the rider can leave the control of his horse to another, and can concentrate on his position, but he will only do this and ride without tension if he has complete confidence in the person doing the lungeing and if the horse is suitable. (This chapter is limited to giving guidance on how to establish a rider's basic position by riding on the lunge without stirrups. The technique of lungeing a horse without a rider differs considerably and is dealt with in Chapter 9, which also covers in more detail the facilities and tack required for lungeing.)

There will come a time when the novice rider will wish to dispense with the lunge and to start riding, using reins and stirrups, and controlling his horse. This is acceptable once the rider has acquired a stable seat, and is the next step in his education. The means by which control is exercised are discussed in Chapters 5 and 6.

But even after the beginner has dispensed with the lunge and can control his own horse, riding without stirrups is still a most useful way of developing the correct position in the saddle. Many advanced riders do much work without stirrups, finding that they are more in harmony with their horse and so more effective. Lungeing a rider of any level is always helpful as it allows the rider to work on his position, suppleness, balance and feel.

RESPONSIBILITIES OF THE INSTRUCTOR

Instructing the rider on the lunge

Anyone undertaking the lungeing of a rider should be well versed in lungeing and sufficiently knowledgeable to be able to correct the rider's position and help him to maintain it at all gaits. The instructor is responsible for modifying the horse's gaits and transitions to suit the rider. Sometimes he may use an assistant to lead the horse and give confidence to or support a novice in the first stages of riding on the lunge.

The rider's safety

When lungeing a rider, the instructor is entirely responsible for his safety and must do everything possible to avoid anything untoward happening which could reduce the rider's confidence. Only if a rider can work without tension will work on the lunge be of value. An instructor should pay attention to the following points, all of which have a bearing on the horse's and rider's safety:

- Lungeing should be carried out in a satisfactory environment (see next page).
- Tack should be strong and well fitted.
- The lunge horse should be suitable.
- Lessons should not be too long and must contain rest periods.

- Instructor, rider and horse should be correctly turned out. The instructor should always wear gloves when handling a lungeing rein, and should discard his spurs. The rider should wear breeches and boots or jodhpurs and must wear a hard hat.

FACILITIES NEEDED

The lungeing area

Lungeing should always be carried out in a reasonably quiet place so that neither the horse's nor the rider's attention is distracted and the instructor's commands can be clearly heard by both. The going must be good. The whole area should be level and, if possible, should be enclosed as this will greatly increase a novice rider's confidence and help the horse's concentration. It follows that an indoor riding school is often an ideal site for a lesson but it is certainly not essential.

An outdoor area can be marked off by use of straw bales, poles and jump stands or the like.

Tack

The tack needed when lungeing a horse and rider consists of:

- A snaffle bridle. The reins can be twisted around under the neck and the throatlash put through one of the loops (see illustration, page 77), but it is safer to knot the reins on the horse's neck once the rider is mounted so that the rider can pick them up in an emergency.

- A cavesson. This is fitted over or under the bridle and buckled under the chin like a drop noseband, or above the bit like cavesson noseband, with the lunge rein fastened to the central swivel ring on the noseband. The noseband and cheek strap must be tightened sufficiently to prevent them pulling round or rubbing the horse's outside eye.

- A lunge rein. About 10m (33ft) long, made of linen webbing or nylon, with a large loop at one end and a swivel joint, attached to a buckle or spring clip, at the other.

Training on the lunge. The depth of the seat and the rider's feel can be improved by selective work without stirrups and/or reins. Here the rider's stirrups are safely crossed in front of the saddle, the reins are secured by a knot, and the rider has one hand on the pommel of the saddle.

- Side-reins. These are about 2m (6ft) long and must be used with caution and only fastened to the bit after the pupil has mounted, and removed before he dismounts. They should run horizontally from the girth about half way up the horse's sides to mouth. (For the correct length see page 80.) When not in use they should be clipped to the Ds of the saddle.
- A saddle. It is important for the saddle to fit both horse and rider. The use of a numnah is recommended.
- A lunge whip.
- Brushing boots for all four legs.

The lunge horse

Ideally, the horse to be used by a rider on the lunge should be a specialist at the job, but a lunge horse must do other work if he is not to become thoroughly stale. Temperament is very important and he must be obedient to the human voice – since, on the lunge, this will be the principal aid. The gaits should be comfortable. Circling is a strain on a horse and a fit and mature animal of six or over should be used. The time spent on the lunge should not exceed twenty minutes (excluding rest periods) if the horse is being used actively.

TECHNIQUE FOR LUNGEING A RIDER

The instructor

The instructor stands in the centre of the lungeing circle, which ideally should be between 15m and 20m in size, and drives the horse round him, holding the lunge rein in the hand towards which the horse is moving, and holding the whip in his other hand. Instructors can hold the loop at the end of the lunge rein in either hand. The instructor must concentrate on the rider and on the horse's hindquarters rather than on his forehand. It is important to ensure that the horse describes a true circle; and the instructor should endeavour to stand fairly still, which should be possible if the horse is active and obedient. A trained lunge horse should be obedient to the instructor's voice. The lunge whip should seldom have to be used, but when it is needed the horse should be lightly touched and usually above the hind fetlocks. Whenever the instructor moves closer to the horse, the whip should be reversed, with the thong trailing to the rear.

Length of a lungeing lesson

As already mentioned, a horse being used actively should not be lunged for more than some twenty minutes, excluding rest periods. Frequent rest periods will be needed, since riding without stirrups can be tiring for riders. The horse should be worked equally on each rein.

Preliminary work

Before the start of a lesson, an instructor will often wish to begin by lungeing the horse without a rider, to loosen him up and make sure he is calm and obedient. Many riders like to 'warm up' by riding on the lunge but using their stirrups. Both measures may be used with advantage.

THE LUNGE LESSON

Rider position

The person lungeing and instructing must ensure that the rider takes up and maintains the correct position in the saddle as defined in Chapter 2. The rider, with the horse stationary, places himself in the deepest part of the saddle, with his weight on his seat bones and his legs hanging loosely down against the saddle. To achieve this position, he should take hold of the front of his saddle with both hands and gently pull his seat into the lowest part, making himself as upright as possible, so that a vertical line running from his ear through the point of his shoulder bisects his hip joint and touches the back of the heel. The side-reins should

not be attached until work on the move begins.
The following two points should be particularly noted:

- There should be no deviation from the line: shoulder-hip-heel. A rider sitting on his fork will tend to be in front of the vertical line, and if he transfers his weight from his seat bones to his buttocks the tendency will be for him to be behind this line. (See illustrations on page 24.)
- The inner thigh muscles must be relaxed so that the knee lies sufficiently low on the saddle to enable the rider gradually to gain more security in the correct position.

Exercise to assist in achieving the correct position

The following simple and short exercise may be carried out before starting work, either when halted or at a walk. The movements should never be jerky and the timing must be left to the rider, the exercise being repeated two or three times. The rider, holding the front of the saddle, stretches both legs sideways away from the horse's side. He then allows the legs to relax completely and to fall gently back on to the saddle, the knee being as low as possible, without straining.

Exercise to build confidence

At all three gaits and on both reins the rider can take one hand off the saddle and allow his arm to hang down just behind his thigh for a circle or two. The whole arm should be relaxed, as this exercise should begin to instil in the rider the importance of a relaxed upper arm once he is holding the reins. When he can let go of the saddle, both arms may be dropped together, care being taken that the waist does not collapse or the shoulders become rounded.

Work at the walk

Lungeing the rider at the walk can be used to give confidence to beginners or nervous riders. There is very little upward thrust in the movement of the horse's back, but an active walk will displace the rider's balance on a horizontal and slightly diagonal plane and riders must be taught that this motion must be absorbed through the suppleness of their loins and seat and must not result in a rocking action of the upper body.

Although all exercises that follow can be carried out at the walk, for more experienced riders the walk is best used for checking the rider's position and during rest periods when the rider is allowed to sit at ease.

If much work is being carried out in walk, it is essential that the side-reins are long enough not to cause restriction to the normal free movement required by the head and neck in walk.

Sitting to the trot on the lunge

Once in the correct position at the walk and with the rider still holding the saddle if required, the horse can be sent quietly forward into a trot, as long as the speed, action and spring of it is well within the rider's capabilities. Advanced riders will be able to cope with more activity and scope in the trot than will novice riders. The rider should concentrate on maintaining their own position with tone but without gripping. Only when the seat and balance are fully established should the rider be encouraged to learn to use the seat to control the movement and action of the horse. At the sitting trot, the rider should adjust to the two-time rhythm of the trot and, remaining supple and with tone, allow the weight of the straight body to sink softly down into the saddle as each pair of diagonal legs meets the ground; horse and rider will then rebound as one during the periods of suspension. Once the rider has achieved this, he will be able to sit still in relation to the movement of his horse.

Rising to the trot on the lunge

Rising to the trot without stirrups has little to commend it, except as a strengthening exercise for jumping and racing. Should a rider need to improve his technique, the stirrups should therefore be re-attached and the leathers so adjusted that he can make and easily retain contact, with the widest part of his foot on the iron and with the heel lower than the toe. It is important to adapt the length of leather to suit the rider's position and not the other way round. If the leathers are too short, either tension will develop – especially in the knees and ankles – or, more likely, the rider will move his seat back in the saddle. If too long, the rider will constantly be dropping his toes to make contact with the irons, so weakening his whole position.

Once the stirrups are the correct length and the horse is moving in a soft, springy trot the rider should allow this action gently to lift his seat bones from the saddle on every diagonal stride. To compensate for this movement the body should also go slightly forward from the top of the hip bones. Retaining this position the rider then sinks softly back into the saddle on the next stride. The feeling should be of 'going forward and down and not up in the air and back' (de Nemethy). The whole movement should be initiated by the action of the horse and not by the rider.

Changing the diagonal

When rising to the trot on the lunge the rider should rise in time with and as the horse's outside shoulder goes forward, thus returning to the saddle as that leg and the inside hind leg hit the ground. This is known as rising on, or using, the outside diagonal, which not only makes it easier for the horse to maintain his balance on the circle but also prevents one-sided muscular development. It also has an important part to play in the use of the aids once the horse is off the lunge. Riders should be encouraged constantly to change the diagonal by sitting down for one additional stride before rising again until they can tell instinctively which diagonal they are using.

Cantering on the lunge

The difficulties entailed when riding at a canter on the lunge are greater than at the walk or trot and this should never be attempted without an experienced, well-balanced, educated horse and an experienced instructor in charge, using a quiet place away from other horses and possible distractions.

Centrifugal force is more noticeable at the canter, and riders should guard against the use of grip to maintain their position. The upper body should not rock in rhythm with the changing horizontal levels of the horse's back; this should be absorbed through supple loins and seat. Not all exercises can be carried out at the canter, and the suitable ones are mentioned in the following paragraphs.

Canter work on the lunge with a rider is extremely demanding, physically, on the horse and therefore its use should be limited.

MOUNTED EXERCISES ON THE LUNGE

When a rider has the confidence and ability to let go of the saddle and to ride easily while maintaining the correct position without gripping, for about five minutes on each rein, further mounted exercises should be attempted. These are designed to improve the rider's position, suppleness and balance and, in the case of the novice, to increase his confidence.

The following general points apply to all exercises on the lunge whether at the walk, trot or canter, and should be observed by the rider and the person lungeing him or supervising the exercise:

- As the basis of riding is rhythm, all exercises should be carried out rhythmically in time with the horse.
- The exercises should develop balance, suppleness and strength without producing tension anywhere.
- The movement of one part of the body should not be reflected in another part.
- Breathing should be deep and controlled with a slight emphasis on exhalation, as this helps relaxation. No exercise in the saddle should make the pupil out of breath.

- All exercises should be carried out on both reins. Few riders sit in an identical position on each side and most have a tendency to twist in the saddle, causing one leg to move forward and the other slightly back.
- Twenty minutes excluding rest periods should be the maximum for work on the lunge for any but the most experienced riders.

The following exercises are suitable for riders on the lunge:

- **Correcting the position.** The rider holds the front of his saddle, keeps his seat firmly in the saddle as he straightens his body upwards at the same time as pulling gently down into the saddle and stretching down with both legs, i.e. there should be an upward and downward correction. This should be done immediately prior to transitions and is a useful exercise at other times. Later the muscle influence of these movements is used to warn the horse that something is about to be asked of him and to ensure that the rider is in the correct position to apply the aids. The rider should develop the habit of correcting his position before asking anything of the horse.

  As the rider progresses, the same exercise may be carried out with the hands in the rein position: i.e. holding imaginary reins, great care being taken that the correct position is not lost, particularly during transitions.

- **Shoulder-shrugging exercise.** Here the object is to remove any tension from the shoulders and the base of the neck. Both shoulders are drawn up as high as possible towards the ears (taking care not to tilt the head back or stick the elbows out), and then allowed to drop back into place. They must not be lowered hesitantly or pulled down forcibly. This act should be repeated five or six times; it must be done in an easy rhythm and without setting up any tension in the back or arms.

- **Head and neck exercises.** The object is to rid the neck and jaw of tension. These exercises are a logical follow-on from the previous one.

  1. The head is allowed to turn steadily anti-clockwise and then clockwise. Care should be taken that the head does not tilt.

  2. Without raising the chin, the head is rolled steadily first to one side and then the other, with the ear as nearly as possible resting on the shoulders, which must not be allowed to lift.

  3. The head is allowed to roll steadily forward until the chin is resting on the chest. Care should be taken that the back does not become rounded.

NB Exercises 1 and 3 should be performed at the halt only.

- **Arm and shoulder exercises.** The object is to flatten and stretch the muscles of the abdomen and free the shoulder joints.

  1. Steadily raise alternate arms with fingers stretched and the elbow joint straight until the arm reaches maximum height with the elbow joint beside the ear, palm facing forward.

  2. Circle the arms slowly to the rear three or four times before returning to normal position. The exercise may then be carried out with both arms simultaneously. The swing should always be backwards and in rhythm with the horse's stride. No force should be used or effort made to complete a full backward circle.

  3. Instead of circling the arms backwards, they may be moved backwards as far as they will go without strain, keeping the arm and fingers straight. The arm is then returned to the vertical position. In both 2 and 3 the shoulder and hip joints must remain parallel.

  4. Raise the arms so that they are horizontal. Turn the body from the waist alternately to the left and the right, while maintaining the arms on the horizontal and at 180° to each other. The seat must remain still. This can be done at the walk and trot.

- **Spine and hip joints.** The object of these exercises is to make the spine and hip joints supple.

  1. Arm turning. Allow the arms to hang limply down and place one hand on the horse's withers and the other over the back of the saddle. Change position by twisting from the waist without losing correct position or the rhythm of the gait. The seat must not move in the saddle nor the backward arm be taken beyond the line of the horse's spine. This exercise may be safely carried out at the halt, walk or trot, but the pupil should be competent and confident before attempting it at the canter.

  2. Jockey position. While holding the front of the saddle, draw the legs up, closing the angles of the ankles, knees and hips, and come forward with the body into the racing position. At first, maintain the position for a few strides but gradually hold for longer and longer. This can be done at the walk and trot.

  3. Scissors. Lengthen legs and while maintaining seat bones in the saddle alternately swing one leg back and the other forwards. This can be done at the walk and trot.

  4. Touching toes. Take one hand and touch the toe on the opposite side. Repeat with the other hand. This exercise should be done in halt, with the instructor at the horse's head.

- **Ankle exercise.** Turn the ankles in as full a circle as possible, firstly clockwise and then anti-clockwise. This can be done at all paces.

CHAPTER

CANTERING, JUMPING AND RIDING OUT

RIDER FITNESS

Every rider must be reasonably fit if he is to be able to maintain the correct position in the saddle, to assist his horse and to enjoy his riding. It is a surprising fact that the energy consumed in riding is of the same order as that used in such obviously physically demanding sports as running or cycling, so that even a novice requires a degree of basic fitness. For the advanced and the competitive rider, such as the jockey, three-day eventer, show jumper or dressage rider, a much higher standard of physical fitness is needed.

Methods of achieving fitness

While daily riding is in itself a good way of keeping fit, it is certainly not enough to reach the standard of fitness required for competition. For this, the rider's heart and lungs must work efficiently, and the muscles of the back and leg should be in particularly good condition. He or she must be supple throughout the body, and excess fat must be avoided.

It is generally agreed that the best way to keep fit is to run regularly, although skipping, swimming and cycling are all useful aids to fitness. There are also many more mounted exercises suitable for riders of all stages; dismounted exercises and yoga, which help as well as promote suppleness and coordination. Many riders have found a study of the Alexander Technique extremely helpful in improving their riding abilities.

It is most important not to overdo physical training, which should always be progressive and should take into account the rider's age and medical condition. In special cases, medical advice should be sought before a strenuous course of training is undertaken.

LEARNING TO CANTER

The horse canters in three-time. The sequence of legs is: outside hind, inside hind and outside fore in a diagonal pair, then inside fore (often referred to as the 'leading leg'). In the canter, the level of the horse's body alters from front to rear. The rider must therefore adjust to this alteration in the levelness of the horse as well as absorbing the up and down spring. The rider must absorb the bounding movement of the canter with his loins and seat and not by swinging his upper body backwards and forwards – which is a very common fault. The hip joints need to be pressed forward, the shoulders remaining on the vertical (not forward) and square to the horse's shoulders. The loins move to follow the undulating movement of the canter. The three hoof beats should be felt. The rider must retain a balanced seat, not slipping to one side of the saddle. Some riders press the hip joint corresponding to the leading leg slightly more forward than the other: i.e. if the near is leading, then the left seat bone should be forward. The rider's legs must remain long, with the inside leg beside the girth and the outside slightly further back. There must be no drawing up of either leg.

The first canter lesson is, for many, a milestone in learning to ride. When you have achieved confidence and some balance in rising and sitting trot, and can ride a little without stirrups, then it is time to try canter. You should learn on a horse that moves smoothly into canter without running into it from an unbalanced trot. Your first canter should probably involve simply moving into canter in a corner (after the short side of the school), travelling down one long side of the school and moving back into trot before the next corner. This will enable you to feel the pace and begin to deal with the increased feeling of speed and the difference in how you must sit.

Your horse will be able to move more easily into canter if you give him the aids on a corner. Sitting tall and staying relaxed, give him the following aids: apply the inside leg on the girth to maintain the forward energy; position the outside leg a little behind the girth to ask him to move into canter on the correct leading leg (see also pages 64–65); with the inside rein ask for a little bend in the direction of the corner; and use the outside rein to control the speed of the trot and regulate the amount of bend.

Once in canter try to relax and allow your seat to slide along the saddle (or 'polish' it), from the back to the front; this will help prevent you from bouncing.

In the downward transition to trot, sit tall and try to follow the movement back into a rising trot rhythm. As you develop confidence and competence you will be able to canter for longer and around the corners of the school; you will also learn how to sit into the downwards transition into trot.

Giving yourself time to learn how to master the canter is the most important criterion here, closely followed by practice and patience.

THE JUMPING POSITION

When jumping, or indeed when galloping on the flat, the rider must modify the basic seat, already described, partly to maintain his balance but also to take his weight off the horse's back.

To adopt the jumping position (also known as the balanced seat, the light seat, and poised position) the rider:

- Shortens his stirrup leathers (the length depending on the work to be carried out), which closes the angles of the hips-knees-ankles.

The light seat/ jumping position.

Development of the light seat for galloping/cross-country.

Positions from the stride before take-off, to the landing.

- Inclines his body forward from the pelvis, which allows the seat to slide back a little (the seat may vary in its contact with the saddle) but at faster paces and when jumping more weight should be taken into the stirrup and so off the horse's back, thus making the seat lighter.
- Increases the weight on the thigh, knee and inside of the stirrup.
- Turns his toes slightly out so as to close the leg muscles around the horse.
- Remains looking forward and with his back flat.
- Holds his hands well in front of him, generally with a shorter rein, in a straight line from the elbow through the forearm, hands and rein to the mouth; the elbows may leave the sides, as they move forward.
- The heel is the deepest part of the position, with the lower leg securely under the rider's body to maintain balance.

The result is that the rider's weight is taken off the horse's back and the rider is able to stay in balance when travelling at speed.

The position in movement when jumping

The jumping position described above is the one generally taught to riders. The position at the various stages of jumping a fence are:

- **The approach.** The approach is made in the basic jumping position described above, making sure that the angle of the body is not more than approximately 45° in front of the vertical. The seat bones may be just clear of, brushing, or lowered into, the saddle. Care must be taken not to get in front of or behind the movement when riding the last stride, but to stay in balance. This is particularly important with young or green horses.

- **The take-off.** Depending on the size of the fence, the angle of the rider's body to the horse is closed, bringing the chest nearer to the mane. This must not be overdone nor must the angle of the knee be opened excessively. The knee must always be forward, pointed, and deep in the saddle. The rein contact is lightened and the hands follow the movement of the horse's head and neck. The lower leg should remain in the same position during this phase and throughout the jump.

- **In mid-air.** Over the top of the fence the rider maintains this position.

- **The descent.** On the descent the body remains inclined forward, and although the seat bones may brush the saddle, there should be no weight on them.

- **The landing.** The rider brings his body back to the original position with the stride after landing.

Variations of the jumping position

Many competition riders use a more upright jumping seat, adapted from that described on page 42. The difference between the positions is one of degree, and experienced riders should be able to adapt their position between more upright and forward as necessary. The essential factor is to **maintain a balanced seat**. In the more upright position, the stirrup leathers may be longer, the amount varying according to the rider's conformation and suppleness. The seat bones rest on the saddle but the main weight is borne by the inside of the thigh and knee.

The body is upright, or nearly upright, but **never** behind the vertical. The hands are well in front of the rider, with the elbows slightly in front of the top of the hips (the iliac crests). There is a straight line from the elbow, through the forearm, hand and rein, to the mouth.

The more upright position enables the rider to control his horse's impulsion and stride better when coming into a fence and on landing. Horses who are lazy or likely to refuse may be more easily controlled from this position; but it requires considerably more expertise and agility on the rider's part if he is not to be left behind the movement with possible damage to the horse's back. It is usually advisable to 'ride in' in the basic jumping position, especially on a young horse, as it takes the weight off the horse's back.

Common position faults in jumping.

'behind the movement'

'in front of the movement'

Variations in the light seat. The amount of weight in the seat to the lower leg varies but the principle remains the same.

Fast work – strong canters and galloping

In fast work on the flat the rider must take care that:

- The stirrups are short enough: otherwise the rider tends to stand in his stirrups and open the angle of the knee. The result is that the seat bones are not close enough to the saddle.
- The rider's body is not too far forward, i.e. the angle is not more than 45° from the vertical.
- The reins are shortened to ensure the rider's hands are well in front of the body.
- See illustration on page 42.

HACKING OUT

As the competence and confidence of the rider develops, hacking out can be a most enjoyable way of putting new-found skills into practice 'in the field'. In the early stages it is essential to hack on a well-mannered horse that is well within the rider's level of ability. Hacking out for the first time can feel a bit like swimming out of your depth. You have to believe in your ability to cope when there are no safe walls to confine you, or, in the case of swimming, nowhere to put your feet down. It is wise to hack out in pairs or groups, and this usually adds to the enjoyment.

If hacking alone, always make sure that someone is aware of where you are going and roughly how long you are likely to be gone. Take some money with you, and perhaps a mobile phone, which you can rely on in the event of an emergency. When riding out by yourself take a familiar route on a horse you have hacked out before.

Depending on the area in which you live, there are some beautiful parts of the countryside accessible to riders – bridle paths, Forestry Commission land, and beaches can all be potential riding areas. Some forestry land may require the rider to hold a current annual pass for access. If you live in the locality this information should be easily obtainable.

Bridle paths often traverse farm land, common land or moorland. Whatever the case, the rider has responsibility in all instances of off-road riding to respect gates and access points and close them as appropriate. Riders must take great care when crossing fields which have livestock in them. The bridle path will often stay close to the perimeter or headland of the field, and this must be adhered to. Cross occupied fields at a slow pace – usually walk – to avoid disturbing the animals. It is essential not to frighten livestock, particularly in-lamb ewes or milking cows, and cause them to 'run' – serious damage or even loss of life can result, for which the rider would be liable.

Awareness of the countryside can be raised and knowledge enhanced by hacking out; it also helps in developing greater skill and confidence as a rider. Experiencing differing terrain and gradients, coupled with the feeling of the greater power that the horse may give through being unconfined and in wide open spaces, should all increase the rider's ability and enjoyment. It is essential, however, that an experienced rider is always in charge of one or more less competent riders, so that confidence and authority can continue to emanate from the leader. If a number of less experienced riders are taken out for a hack then it is advisable to have more than one competent escort.

Hacking out can range from a simple hour's ride around a local loop, to a longer ride of several hours' duration. In the latter case it is more important to plan the route carefully and perhaps involve a stop at a friendly pub for lunch or a snack. If long rides are planned, the riders and the horses must be fit enough, and perhaps would need to take some precautions against changeable or inclement weather. Riding out for longer than a day can become a challenging and enjoyable holiday option at home or abroad.

Roadwork

Many horsemen over decades have ridden on roads to develop their horses' stamina, fitness and to harden/strengthen their legs. Historically, before the modern age of motorised transport, coach horses travelled the countryside in all directions, completing many miles in one work period. These days, many riders still use roadwork for fittening and recreational purposes, although for the latter many new aspects must be seriously considered.

Many of today's roads are heavily overloaded with traffic, and certainly the main arterial routes are totally unsuitable for recreational riding. While country roads remain much quieter, every rider needs to be aware of the potential dangers of riding horses on the road.

Today's cars are fast and powerful, and drivers often in too much of a hurry to reach their destination. Many drivers, particularly, those from urban areas, have no experience of horses and are totally unaware of the hazards involved in meeting one or more horses on the road.

If a rider is going to ride on the road, either for fittening, pleasure or to connect bridleways or other off-road riding routes, then certain precautions need to be taken to try to ensure safety. It is absolutely vital that horses taken on the road are traffic-proof. Most horses, through careful introduction and training, will learn to accept cars and other vehicles in a calm way. The early training must initially involve the young horse seeing vehicles in his home environment – for example, cars in the yard, perhaps the farrier's van or a tractor used for harrowing the fields or arena. From accepting these vehicles, the young horse should then be hacked on quiet roads on the inside or behind a schoolmaster who is very reliable on the road and with traffic. The youngster will then learn to tolerate vehicles passing him as he takes his example from the lead horse.

A few horses find heavy traffic (e.g. tractors and lorries) altogether too frightening and try to turn and run away from such horrors. From experience, most horses that react in this way do so because of an earlier unfortunate confrontation on the road, giving reason to their fears. In the interests of safety, it is recommended that unreliable horses are not taken onto the road.

The rider himself also needs to develop experience and confidence on the road. Nervous riders make nervous horses, and the combination is dangerous. If a rider has an intrinsic fear of roadwork then he is better staying in an arena or in off-road situations. Initial road riding should be in the company of an experienced rider on a safe, confident horse.

The rider must learn his responsibilities as a road user. One of the best ways to do this is to train for and take the British Horse Society Riding and Road Safety Test. Preparation for and attainment of the certificate of competence will educate the rider in all aspects of roadcraft and safety. A comprehensive booklet entitled 'Riding and Roadcraft', published by the British Horse Society, contains all the relevant information.

As a road user on a horse, just as in a vehicle, courtesy and consideration for other road users leads to harmony and understanding between all participants.

In conclusion:

- safe off-road riding is the ideal place for recreational riding;
- roadwork is still a viable option for riding in certain parts of the countryside;
- roadwork is still regarded by many as an essential part of fittening competition horses.

Riding up and down hills

Riding up and down hills requires balance and feel from the rider so that he can assist the horse in negotiating the gradient. As the rider develops more security in his position he will be better able to cope with differing terrain when riding out or hacking.

It is usually easier to adapt to riding up or down hill by taking up a slightly shorter stirrup, rather more towards a jumping length. The closed angle between the lower leg and thigh, and that between the thigh and upper body, will better enable the rider to follow the changing balance of the horse as he tackles the up or down slope.

Generally, the steeper the gradient up hill, the more the rider needs to incline the body forward, taking weight off the horse's back. The rider's weight is then concentrated more into the lower leg, leaving the horse the freedom to use his hind legs and his back to

Riding up hill.

Riding down hill.

negotiate the hill. When riding down hill the rider needs to become more upright but without taking more weight into the seat and therefore loading the horse's back.

In hill work the rider must learn to develop a good sense of balance to retain a secure position which is both comfortable and affords a feeling of control, and does not impede the horse's ability to deal with the gradient.

When riding up or down hill the slope should always be ridden straight as this will put less strain on the horse's limbs and joints than if the slope is traversed at an angle (i.e. obliquely).

Opening gates

This can be a very necessary practical task when riding in the countryside or when going from roads to fields or back. As in much of the information given in this book, there is a requirement for both horse and rider to learn how to perform the task and to gain competence through practice. It is essential that you leave any gate secured in the way you found it, particularly if there are stock in the fields.

Gates can be opened mounted or dismounted. Usually the choice is governed by how securely the gate is fastened and how awkward it is to handle from the horse's back.

Opening a gate – mounted

(This example assumes the gate is on your right and opens away from you.) Position the horse alongside/parallel to the gate, with his head just past the opening end of the gate. Putting the reins (and whip if carried) into the left hand, lean forward and down to unfasten the gate with your right hand. Using your right leg behind the girth, move the horse's hindquarters over and push the gate open as he moves sideways.

If you are letting other riders through, once the gate is wide enough, ask the horse to stand still as you keep the gate open to allow the ride to pass. Either keeping hold of the gate, or pushing it away wide, take your horse quietly through the gate making sure that if the gate is free it doesn't swing closed and catch the horse on his hindquarters. Then catch the gate or control it to close it, and again position the horse parallel to the gate while you secure the latch.

Opening a gate – dismounted

Sometimes it is impossible to open a gate from the horse's back. The gate may need lifting, it may be fixed

Opening and closing a gate (see text).

by a securely tied rope or there may an unwieldy chain at an awkward height. In such cases dismounting is a necessity.

If in a group, make sure that other riders give you space to manoeuvre – your horse must not be at risk of being kicked or trodden on by others close by. If the area is confined with, say, overhanging branches, pull your stirrups over the front of the saddle as you dismount, to prevent them being caught on anything. (This is a wise precaution and a useful habit to adopt under many circumstances.)

Whether you take the reins over the horse's head or leave them around his neck will depend on: (a) whether the horse is wearing a running martingale or not; (b) how much room there is to manoeuvre; and (c) how cooperative and biddable the horse is.

If the horse is wearing a martingale, there is not much space and the horse is very leadable, then leave the reins around the neck. Deal with the gate while holding the horse, and then carefully push him back or sideways using your voice and hand pressure to enable you to open the gate wide. As before, allow other riders through while keeping your horse still and out of the way of passing horses.

Once through, the other riders should stay close to the gate and should not start to move off, otherwise your horse might become fretful, thinking he is being left behind. Secure the gate, remount, take back your stirrups and reins, and then inform the group that you are ready to proceed.

CHAPTER

THE THEORY OF THE AIDS

Aids are the language of horsemanship and, like all languages, have a basic structure, but it is emphasis and timing which lend them expression and refinement. It is essential that anyone who wishes to ride well should understand the use, the reasons for, and the effect of the aids, before he tries to teach them to his horse. The horse must be taught stage by stage and with complete clarity until the rapport between rider and horse is built up to such a level that it appears that the rider has but to think for the horse to obey willingly. This is the essence of true horsemanship. A trainer who can combine intelligence with mental and physical control and coordination can produce a highly trained, alert and happy horse, working with ease and with complete confidence in his rider.

Definition and types of aid

An aid is the signal or means by which a rider conveys his wishes to his horse. It refers to any action by the rider which results in physical or mental communication between him and his horse.

Aids are sub-divided into natural and artificial as follows:

- **Natural aids**. The rider's voice, legs, seat and hands.
- **Artificial aids**. Whips, spurs and any form of strap (other than the reins) which control or position the horse, with or without the rider's help. Examples are standing or running martingales, draw or running reins. Only the whip and spur have a place in classical equitation and are the only artificial aids considered in this chapter.

NATURAL AIDS

The voice

The voice by its tone can encourage, correct, soothe or reward. It is also used to give commands, particularly on the lunge and with a young horse when it is first ridden. The horse learns that sharp, quick commands 'walk on', 'trot', 'canter' mean to go forward, and slow and drawn-out 'whoa', 'wa-alk','ter-rot' to reduce the pace. Intonation of the voice upwards for a transition to a faster pace (e.g. from trot to canter) and downwards for a transition to a slower pace (e.g. trot to walk) will add further authority to the aid.

The legs, seat and hands

Although they are discussed separately below, the legs, seat and hands are always used in conjunction with one another as explained in the next chapter.

The legs

The major functions are:

- To create forward movement.

- To activate the hindquarters.
- To indicate direction and to control the position of the horse.
- To move the horse laterally (sideways).

Identical use of the legs

The effect of using both legs by the girth is to encourage the horse to move forward. When first handled, any horse will react to human contact by withdrawing from it. As flight is his natural defence, when first mounted and feeling the legs of the rider enclosing his rib cage, the reaction is to move forward away from the pressure. This is the basis of all training and is developed and refined by constant repetition, until the slightest pressure with the inside of the rider's leg will result in the horse moving forward.

Individual use of the legs

Once this reaction of moving forward is established, the application of either of the rider's legs by the girth will encourage the horse to move the hind leg forward on that side. Since it will also be instinctive for the horse to try to evade the pressure on the ribs it will also tend to bring the leg forward and slightly under the weight of the body preparatory to turning the hindquarters away from the point of stimulus. This effect is used to move the horse laterally, but if it is not desired, and the horse is required simply to turn a corner, then the rider prevents the hindquarters falling out by placing his other leg slightly further back from the girth. Hence, while both legs cause the horse to go forward, the rider's inside leg by the girth accentuates the forward movement while the outside leg, slightly behind the girth, controls the hindquarters.

Response to the leg aids

The lower legs must always remain in quiet, soft contact with the horse's sides. When a particular signal is required, the legs are used with a vibrant, changing pressure and not a constant squeeze. They should be applied as lightly as possible and only when required, as repeated heavy thumping with the legs, heels or spurs will cause the horse to become dead to the leg.

NB A horse which reacts to leg aids by drawing back is said to be 'behind the leg', and a horse that goes freely forward at the slightest indication from the rider's legs is said to be 'in front of the leg'.

The seat, including the weight

The major influences are on:

- Impulsion.
- Outline.
- Direction.

Use of seat and weight aids

The seat aids can be used beneficially only if the rider can sit correctly, softly and quietly with the weight equally on both seat bones. He must allow the horse to remain supple and to swing his back. The novice rider should concentrate on using his seat only insofar as he allows the horse's movement to go 'through': i.e. he allows the horse's back muscles to operate freely so that the actions of the hindquarters and forehand are coordinated and not separated by a stiff back. Thus the rider should not sit heavily and stiffly, which would suppress the movement 'through' the horse's back and make the outline hollow. A rider can start to use the seat aids when he can feel the actions of the hind legs and his seat is independent enough to be able to apply an aid without setting up undesired changes or movements elsewhere in his body.

These aids can be used in the following ways:

- To lighten the weight on the seat bones and allow the horse's back to come up.
- To allow the horse's back muscles to swing by sitting passively with supple hips.
- To request the desired rhythm.
- In conjunction with the back and lower leg to engage

the hindquarters and bring the hind legs more underneath.

On the young horse the weight must be used with great care: if it is not, the horse will hollow and tighten his back. This is why on a young horse most of the early trot work is done rising and much of the first canter work with the rider in a slightly forward seat, off the horse's back. This is particularly important with Thoroughbreds. On the more trained horse, going in a correct round outline, the weight and the use of the back become very important aids.

On straight lines the rider's weight must be absolutely central.

On turns, circles, lateral work and in canter the weight is brought slightly to the inside by turning the body in the direction of the movement and putting more weight into the inside stirrup.

The hands

The major influences are to:

- Contain the impulsion created by the rider's legs and seat. (Impulsion is the energy created by the activity of the hindquarters.)
- Control the speed.
- Help the balance.
- Indicate direction.
- Control the bend and aid maintenance of outline.

The hands are only supplementary and complementary to the seat and leg aids. The rider should apply the leg (and seat) aids before the hands, otherwise the hindquarters will tend to fall out behind and the impulsion will be lost rather than contained. As already stated, the use of the seat must be gradually established with a very young horse.

Response to hand aids

Through the reins and the bit the hands are a 'telephone' to the horse's brain and their use has a paramount effect on his mental and physical attitude.

To be most effective the hands should:

- Never pull backwards.
- Remain still in relation to the movement of the horse and entirely independent of the action of any other part of the rider's body.
- Maintain a consistent, light, sympathetic but elastic contact with the bit (except when riding on a loose rein). The horse loses his sense of security if the rein contact is inconsistent.
- Keep the same weight in walk, trot and canter, taking care not to make the contact stronger in the faster gaits.

Individual use of the hands

The tension in the reins may not be the same in both hands when working on turns or circles, at the canter, and when correcting the natural crookedness of the horse. It is when working a straight horse on straight lines at the walk and trot that the rider should have an even feel in both hands. For most of the time the reins should be used as follows:

- **Outside hand**. The hand on the opposite side to the rider's inside leg will receive some of the impulsion sent forward from the horse's inside hind leg. To control this the rider maintains a positive contact with the horse, i.e. one that neither releases nor pulls back the rein but maintains a consistent, sympathetic contact in relation to the movement and therefore goes with it.
- **Inside hand**. The inside hand accepts and guides the inside bend of the horse, a bend which is created by the rider's seat and leg aids. The contact should be light and flexible to encourage the relaxation of the horse's lower jaw and the acceptance of the bit.

The principle is that the outside hand maintains a positive contact which controls the pace and assists the balance, while the inside hand is more flexible and indicates the bend.

On a long rein.

On a loose rein.

RIDING ON A LONG AND ON A LOOSE REIN

A horse can be ridden on a long rein, but the rider should maintain impulsion with his legs and seat while allowing the horse to relax and to stretch forward and down with his head and neck and to lengthen his stride. In walk, for example, the rider, by opening his fingers, lets the reins slide as the horse asks for the extra length but does not completely lose contact. This is known as a **free walk on a long rein**.

There are times when a horse is ridden on a loose rein without any contact at all. The only connection between the hand and mouth is through the weight of the rein alone. A **walk on a loose rein**, is ridden in the same way as a walk on a long rein, but all contact with the horse's mouth is abandoned and the horse is kept straight by the use of the rider's seat and legs alone. Work on a long and loose rein may be used at all three gaits, providing impulsion and balance are maintained.

METHODS OF HOLDING THE REINS

There are many different but acceptable methods of holding the reins. Some of the main ones are mentioned and illustrated on the following pages.

In most methods of holding the reins, the reins run from the horse's mouth, through the fingers, across the palm of the hand and out between the thumb and forefinger, with the thumb on top of the rein. The hand must be lightly closed. In all cases it is the pressure of the thumbs on the reins over the forefingers which prevents the reins from slipping, and not the grip of a clenched hand or fingers.

- **Snaffle bridle**. When held in both hands, the reins pass between the third and fourth fingers, across the palm of the hand and out between the first finger and thumb; alternatively, the reins go round the outside of the little finger and out between the first finger and the thumb. When held in one hand, the most commonly used methods are to put the rein being moved between the thumb and first finger and out at the bottom of the hand, or to put it between the second or third finger and out between the first finger and thumb.

- **Double bridle**. When held in both hands, three recommended methods are:

1. The bridoon rein passes outside the little finger, and the Weymouth rein, between the third and little finger. Both reins then cross the palm of the hand and go out between the first finger and thumb. This

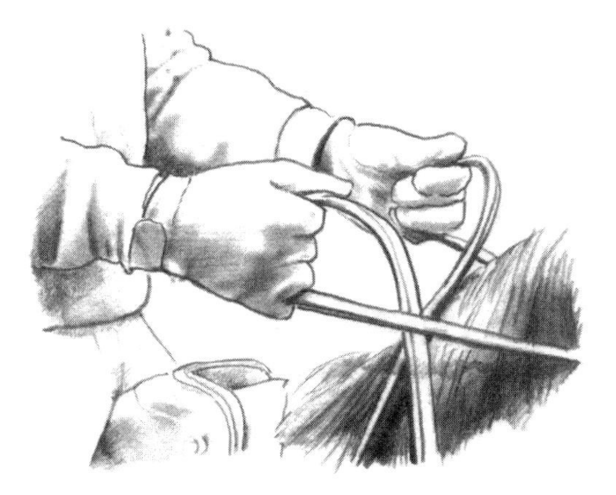

Snaffle reins held in both hands.

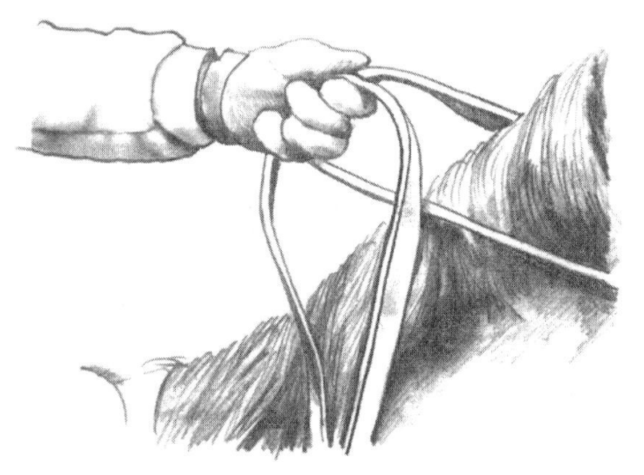

Snaffle reins held in one hand.

is the most usual way of holding the reins of a double bridle.

2. As in 1 above, except that the position of the bridoon and Weymouth reins are reversed.

3. Both bit reins are held in one hand, separated by the second or third finger. The bridoon rein, on that side, passes outside the little finger. All three reins pass out between the first finger and thumb. The other bridoon rein is held between the fingers of the other hand.

The bit reins are adjusted to the required length on taking them up between the fingers and thereafter are not altered, the horse being ridden on the bridoon reins in each hand.

Should the rider wish to hold the reins in one hand: e.g. the left hand, he has only to transfer the right snaffle rein to the left hand, placing it over the top of the index finger and allowing the slack to hang down from the palm.

The most usual way of holding the reins of a double bridle.

An alternative method of holding the reins of a double bridle. Here the position of the bridoon and Weymouth reins are reversed.

THE ARTIFICIAL AIDS

The whip

The whip helps to reinforce the leg aids should they prove insufficient. It should be used quickly and lightly behind the leg to emphasise the aid or to ask for more attention.

On occasion it will be necessary to change the hand in which the whip is held. The procedure with a long schooling whip is to put the reins into the hand holding the whip, and the free hand then takes hold of the whip below the holding hand, the back of the hand towards the rider's body. The whip is brought quietly across to the other side with the tapered end of the whip passing in front of the rider's face; the rein is then retaken by the whip hand.

An alternative method, and one that is more appropriate for a short 'jumping type' whip, is to put the reins into the hand holding the whip; then the free hand takes hold of the whip above the holding hand, and draws it through the hand. The whip is then brought quietly across to the other side, tapered end downwards. The reins are then picked up again.

The **schooling whip** is used for schooling on the flat. It should be between 0.90 m (3ft) and 1.2m (4ft) so that it is long enough to apply without taking the hand off the rein. The wrist is flicked to result in a tickle or a tap

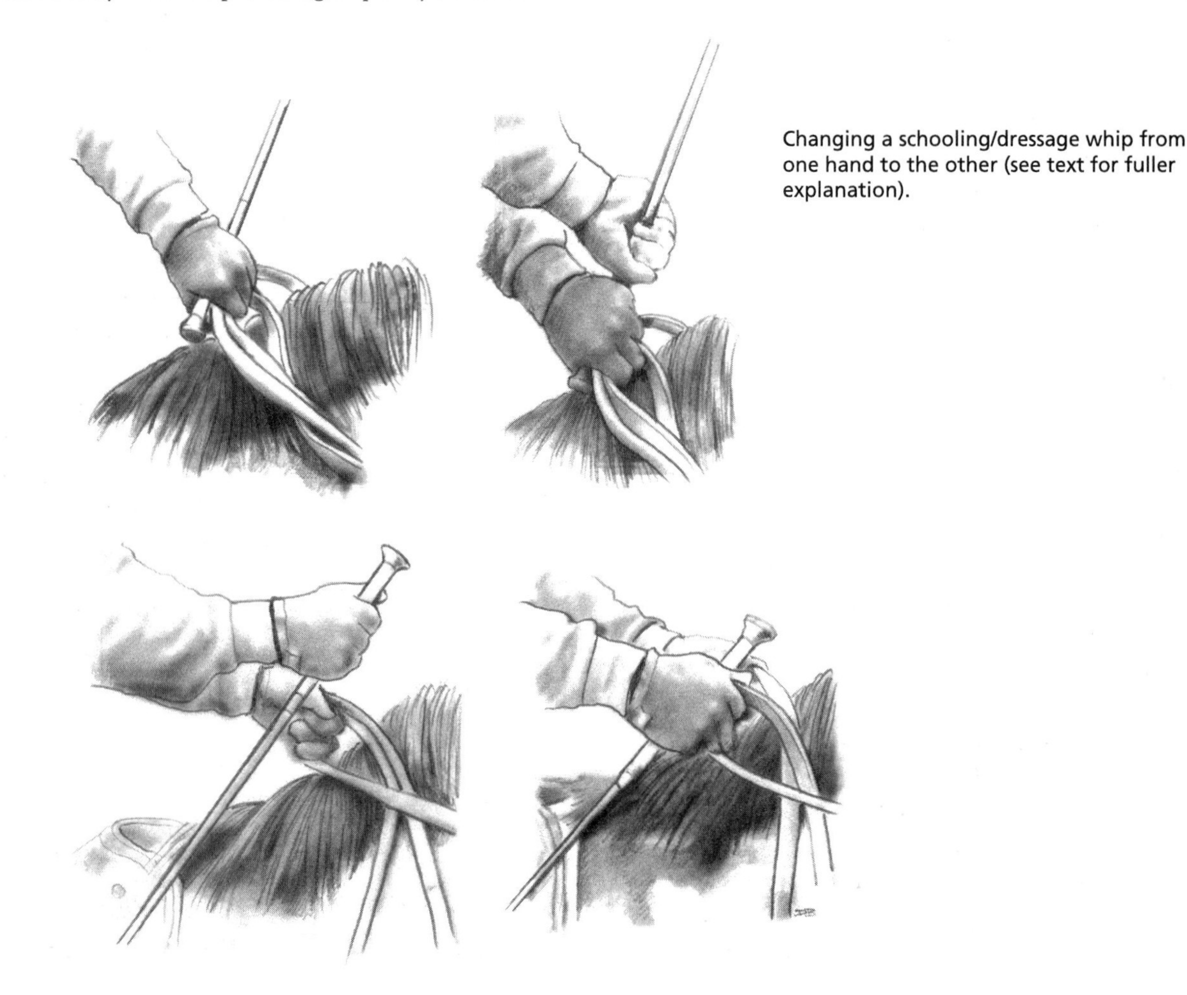

Changing a schooling/dressage whip from one hand to the other (see text for fuller explanation).

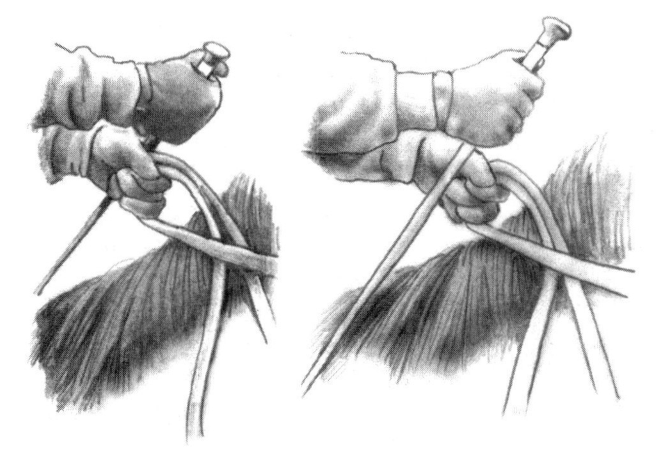

Changing a short whip from one hand to the other (see text for fuller explanation).

whenever required, behind the rider's leg.

The **shorter whip**, used for jumping, must not exceed 75cm (30in.). The whip hand should be taken off the rein, and both reins should be held in one hand and the whip applied behind the leg. The rider should practise this action and the ability to change whip hands with each type of whip.

Spurs

Spurs are regarded as an artificial aid in the same category as the whip. They may be introduced when the horse has accepted the concept of reacting to the leg aid and should permit a more refined reaction to the leg. It is important that the rider's position is secure and independent, and that he can fully control the application of his legs. Spurs are rarely used in the early training of a horse and are not suitable for use by inexpert horsemen.

The spur position on the back of the rider's boot, in the region of the ankle joint, should enable a light aid to be given on the horse's flank, as required. When used the spur should only brush the skin. At no stage should the spur be constantly jabbing at the horse's side, with the rider's leg gripping on. In this case the spur could mark or damage the horse's side, which would be unacceptable and abusive.

Spurs are a refinement of the aids and should not be used as a sole means of creating impulsion. The rider must be able to apply his legs without the spurs touching the horse.

Whilst spurs are mandatory in dressage competitions of medium level and above, they are optional at lower levels. Much depends on the horse's natural responsiveness to the aids. Lazy horses can benefit from being ridden in spurs. Sometimes, though, it is wise to vary the times when spurs are worn (e.g. not always when schooling) so that the horse stays lively to their use.

Spurs vary in size and severity – some are very small, smooth and rounded, whilst others are longer, more angular or with rowels. Restrictions on certain types of spur are made in some competitions, so check the rules before competing.

PRACTICAL USE OF THE AIDS

The aids and movements can be used in every form of riding. The horse will often be required to carry out some of the schooling movements, not merely as an exercise, or part of a dressage test, but for strictly practical reasons. For example, when out hacking, besides the obvious necessity of the aids for changing direction or altering pace, the turn on the forehand, the pirouette and the rein-back may be used when opening and closing gates, and a rider can help to prevent the horse from shying by using the shoulder-in.

SUMMARY

- The aim is for the aids to encourage the horse to go forward, straight and with rhythm.
- Ride from the inside leg into the outside rein.
- Use inside leg for impulsion, close to girth.
- Use outside leg for controlling quarters, a little back.

- Use inside rein for direction and bend.
- Use outside rein for balance, controlling pace and regulating bend.
- Keep weight to inside in turns, circles and lateral work.
- Turn body in direction of movement.
- Always keep body upright.

Good aids are those which

- Ensure that the forward impetus of the horse is given willingly and completely into the rider's control.
- Dictate the pace and/or the direction of the movement.
- Are unobtrusive.

Aids are misused if they

- Position or restrain the horse's body or speed by force.
- Create more impulsion than the rider can control.
- Fail to create the impulsion needed to help the horse to accept the bit.
- Fail to allow the rider's weight to move in harmony with that of the horse.
- Fail to allow the hands to follow the horse's movement.
- Are neither definite nor clear enough for the horse to comprehend their meaning.
- Are used continually, even involuntarily and without reason or anticipation.
- Are used roughly, obviously, or to punish without justification.

CHAPTER

THE USE OF THE AIDS

This chapter describes how the rider uses the aids to convey his wishes to his horse. The aids are comparatively few but the way in which they are applied – for example, the degree of pressure of each leg and of contact in each rein – can vary greatly, and their use calls for skill and tact on the part of the rider.

For the aids to be most effective the rider must be in balance himself, and this is best achieved by establishing the correct position.

Definitions

For fuller definitions of the movements, refer to the British Horse Society's *Rules for Dressage*, and the Fédération Equestre Internationale (FEI) *Rules for Dressage Events*.

The terms '**inside**' and '**outside**' are used frequently and refer to the slight curve throughout the length of the horse's body, 'inside' always being the concave side of the horse when correctly bent, and vice versa; they **do not** refer to the sides of the school or manege.

Forward movement

In all forward movement it is essential for the rider to look ahead at the point towards which he is asking the horse to move.

The first aid used by the rider is to activate the horse's hind legs into forward movement. To achieve this into the walk or trot (often referred to as 'moving off' or 'going forward into'; or into the canter (usually called 'striking off'), or for other upward transitions, the aids are as follows:

Moving off and upward transitions

The rider

- Checks his position.
- Maintains a light contact through the reins with the horse's mouth.
- Applies extra pressure with both legs by the girth – not a steady squeeze but a series of quick, vibrant touches with the inside of his calf muscles.
- Advanced riders, who are able to feel the natural inclination of their horse to favour a left or right bend, may compensate for this when moving off into a faster gait by adopting the opposite position: e.g. position right on a horse with a preference for a left bend. (See 'Position right and left', page 60.) This helps to maintain suppleness and keeps the horse straight.

The halt (see also page 95)

The aids are the same as for all downward transitions,

but in this case the restraining but allowing hands finally stop the movement. Even in the halt impulsion should not be allowed to escape, so the horse maintains a light contact with the bit and the rider's legs remain on the horse's side.

The half-halt (see also page 95)

This is a hardly visible moderated version of the halt - 'the momentary collection of a horse in motion' (Von Blixen-Finecke).

The rider

- Applies momentarily the driving aids of the seat and the legs.
- Restrains momentarily with his hands the horse's consequent desire to go forward so that the horse becomes more collected, rather than going faster.
- Releases momentarily the pressure on the reins before restoring the original contact.
- The horse is enclosed briefly between the weight, leg and rein aids before the hands yield again.
- The half-halt may be repeated as frequently as required to concentrate the energy into the hind legs and increase the horse's desire to go forward more confidently into the bridle.

Controlling the forward movement

The reins are used to control the forward movement, but except in the case of a very young horse their action must be in conjunction with the legs and seat aids in order to keep the hindquarters engaged. These rein aids are applied through sympathetic movement of the fingers and the hands.

It is easy for riders to become over-focused on the contact or weight of the rein. They should aim to remember that the feel in the rein relates directly to the activity from the hind legs!

Downward transitions

The rider

- Checks his position.
- Makes one or more half-halts with the outside rein or with both reins, the former is more acceptable as long as the contact on the inside rein is consistently maintained and the bit is not moved through the horse's mouth.
- Uses the legs and seat to engage the hind legs and lower the quarters so that the horse's forehand is lightened.
- Uses the reins as little as necessary with a restraining but not restrictive movement. The slowing-down aid is usually given with the outside rein.
- As soon as the new gait is established, rides forward by the use of the seat and legs ensuring that the rhythm of that new gait is maintained.
- Takes care that his balance is maintained so that he is not left forward of the movement.

Upward transitions within a pace

For transitions from collected to working, medium or extended gaits:

The rider

- Checks his position.
- Makes a half-halt to get the horse's hind legs more engaged.
- Applies his legs by the girth to lengthen the stride.
- With the reins, while containing the impulsion, allows the horse to lengthen his outline.
- Maintains a supple seat, through movement of his loins and hip joints, thus allowing the horse to swing through his back.

NB At the trot, during training, it is often advisable to rise.

Turns and circles (see also illustration on page 26)

In turns and circles the horse remains bent around the rider's leg. His hind legs should follow exactly in the track of the front legs. This is achieved by riding from the inside leg into the outside rein.

So to turn or circle:

The rider

- Checks his position.
- Applies his fingers on the inside rein intermittently, to establish a more flexible contact and a slight bend, and thus indicate direction.
- Turns his body to the inside and transfers slightly more weight into the inside stirrup.
- Uses the outside rein to allow the bend of the horse's head and neck with a constant contact, unless he brings it into use to control the impulsion and the extent of the bend.
- Uses both legs and a supple seat to maintain impulsion, but the inside leg by the girth dominates and must be sufficiently effective to induce the horse to bring his hind leg, on that side, forward and slightly under the centre of his body; only then will the horse be able to follow the true line of the circle.
- Rests his outside leg slightly back. The leg remains in

Correct bend through the horse's body. Hind leg tracks corresponding foreleg.

this position ready for use if the horse's hindquarters start to swing to the outside of the circle.

- Is very careful not to increase the weight of the inside rein.

Position right and left

A rider is said to be in position right when he has his right leg close to the girth, and his left leg a little behind the girth, therefore indicating a slight bend with the right rein and controlling the impulsion, speed and bend with the left rein. He is then said to be riding from the inside leg into the outside rein. In position left the aids are reversed.

The rider spends much time in position right or left with the need to combat the horse's natural crookedness; also because of the frequency of turns, the action of the horse at the canter, and as a preparation for many movements.

Striking off into canter

The rider

- Checks his position.
- Asks his horse for position right or left according to which leading leg is required. (See pages 64–65.)
- Applies the outside leg back behind the girth to encourage the horse's hind leg on that side to move forward and so to start the sequence of the canter gait (pages 64–65).
- Applies the inside leg by the girth to encourage forward movement.
- Moves the inside seat bone forward, and when the canter is established the weight comes slightly to that inner side.
- Moves the weight a little to the inside.
- Takes care to keep the horse straight and not allow the quarters to move to the inside.

Training the Horse

CHAPTER

THE GAITS

To train a horse correctly it is vital to maintain and improve the purity of the gaits rather than to create or fail to correct the numerous defects which develop in the horse's movements. Therefore, the trainer must understand the way the horse should move at the walk, trot and canter, and for each of these gaits the sequence of the leg movements is different, as is the rhythm of the hoof beats.

THE WALK

Rhythm

Four hoof beats should be heard at equal intervals. The horse moves one leg after another so that the four hoof beats can be heard with the same period between each. Two or three feet are always on the ground at the same time, the horse stepping from one foot to another with no moment of suspension.

Sequence in which the legs leave the ground

Left hind leg: left foreleg; right hind leg; right foreleg.

The aims

- Rhythm of hoof beats is regular with the four beats distinctly marked. Any losses of regular four-time hoof beats are incorrect. This includes a two-time walk (known as a pace or amble).
- The strides are even and not hurried.
- The strides are free, purposeful and unconstrained.
- The head nods in the walk. The rider should not restrict this movement.
- The legs are lifted, not dragged along the ground.

NB Faults in the walk are easily developed, as there is little impulsion to help the rider maintain the rhythm of the pace. It is, therefore, not advisable to walk 'on the bit' during the early stages of training.

The sequence of footfalls at the walk.

THE TROT

Rhythm

Two hoof beats should be heard, with the legs moving in alternate diagonal pairs, but separated by a moment of suspension. This moment of suspension is difficult for the inexperienced rider to sit to, and the problem can be avoided by rising out of the saddle as one of the diagonal pairs leaves the ground and returning to the saddle as this same pair comes back to the ground (rising trot).

Sequence in which legs leave the ground

1. Right foreleg and left hind leg.
2. Left foreleg and right hind leg before the right foreleg and left hind leg touch the ground.

The aims

- The rhythm of the hoof beats are regular (two-time).
- The strides are even in length and not hurried.
- The strides are light and elastic.
- The hindquarters are engaged.
- The joints flex and the limbs are not dragged.
- The hind feet do not hit the forefeet (forging).
- The head remains steady.

The forelegs should not show more extravagant movement than the hind legs.

The sequence of footfalls at the trot.

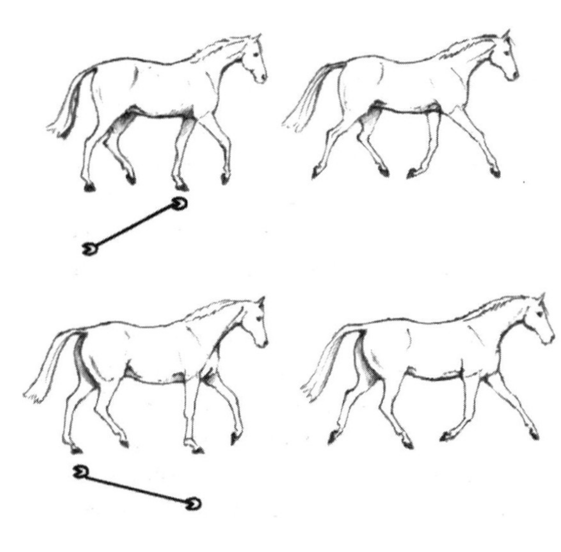

THE CANTER

Rhythm

Three hoof beats should be heard and, as with the trot, there is a moment of suspension when all four feet are off the ground.

Sequence in which legs leave the ground

When the right foreleg leads:

1. Left hind leg
2. Right hind and left foreleg together
3. Right foreleg followed by a moment of suspension.

When the left foreleg leads:

1. Right hind leg
2. Left hind leg and right foreleg together
3. Left foreleg followed by a moment of suspension.

When the canter is **disunited** (a fault) the forehand is on one lead and the hindquarters on the other.

The aims

- Rhythm of hoof beats is regular (three-time). Four hoof beats should not be heard, but they often are when a horse is slowed down without sufficient impulsion.
- Strides are even and not hurried.
- Steps are light and cadenced.
- Hindquarters are engaged with active hocks.
- Balance is maintained.
- Horse is straight, with his shoulders directly in front and not to one side of his hindquarters.
- The canter is true (not disunited).

The sequence of footfalls at right canter.

The sequence of footfalls at left canter.

- Head moves in coordination with the horizontal action of the body. The horizontal movement occurs because when only the leading foreleg is on the ground the hindquarters must rise and the head tip towards the ground, whereas at the end of the moment of suspension the hindquarters drop and the head rises. The result is a bounding action by the horse in the canter.

The aims

- Rhythm of hoof beats is regular (four-time).
- Strides are even and not hurried.
- Balance is maintained although the centre of gravity is more forward.
- Horse is straight with his shoulders directly in front and not to one side of his hindquarters.

THE GALLOP

Rhythm

This is the horse's fastest and most extended gait: the diagonal sequence of the canter is broken. It thus becomes a pace in which four hoof beats should be heard, followed by a moment of suspension.

Sequence in which legs leave the ground

When the left foreleg leads:

1. Right hind leg
2. Left hind leg
3. Right foreleg
4. Left foreleg followed by a moment of suspension.

VARIATIONS WITHIN A GAIT

A horse can be asked to extend and/or collect (that is, change the length of his strides and outline) at each gait. The extent of the variations within a gait depends upon the stage of the horse's training, and on his own natural ability.

In the initial training, the horse has not the impulsion or suppleness to collect or extend truly: therefore at the trot and canter the working gaits only should be asked for, and in the walk just the medium and free walk. As the training proceeds progressively, more collection can be demanded and at the same time extension, to achieve first of all the medium trot and canter and eventually, the extended walk, trot and canter.

Aims within these variations

- The collection should result in shorter, rounder strides not slower ones, and for the extension more ground-covering, longer strides not quicker ones. When trying to extend the strides hurrying is one of the most common faults and leads to stiffening, which can spoil the paces. It is nearly always caused by the rider asking the horse to extend before he has enough impulsion to be able to do so.
- The strides should be even: i.e. when the required length of stride has been achieved each stride should be maintained at this length, so that every stride is even.
- The rhythm of the hoof beats of a particular pace should remain true (the walk four-time, the trot two-time and the canter three-time): i.e. the pace should be regular.
- In all variations within a pace the horse should retain his willingness to go freely forward.

Working gaits

These are the gaits which lie between the collected and medium. They are used particularly for horses not yet trained and ready for collected paces. Working walk is not recognised, but the working trot and canter are the gaits from which respectively other trots and canters are developed.

Aims at all working gaits

- To maintain the balance.
- To keep the horse 'on the bit'.
- For the hocks to be active, but this does not mean collection, only the production of impulsion from active hindquarters.
- To produce strides which are free and elastic.

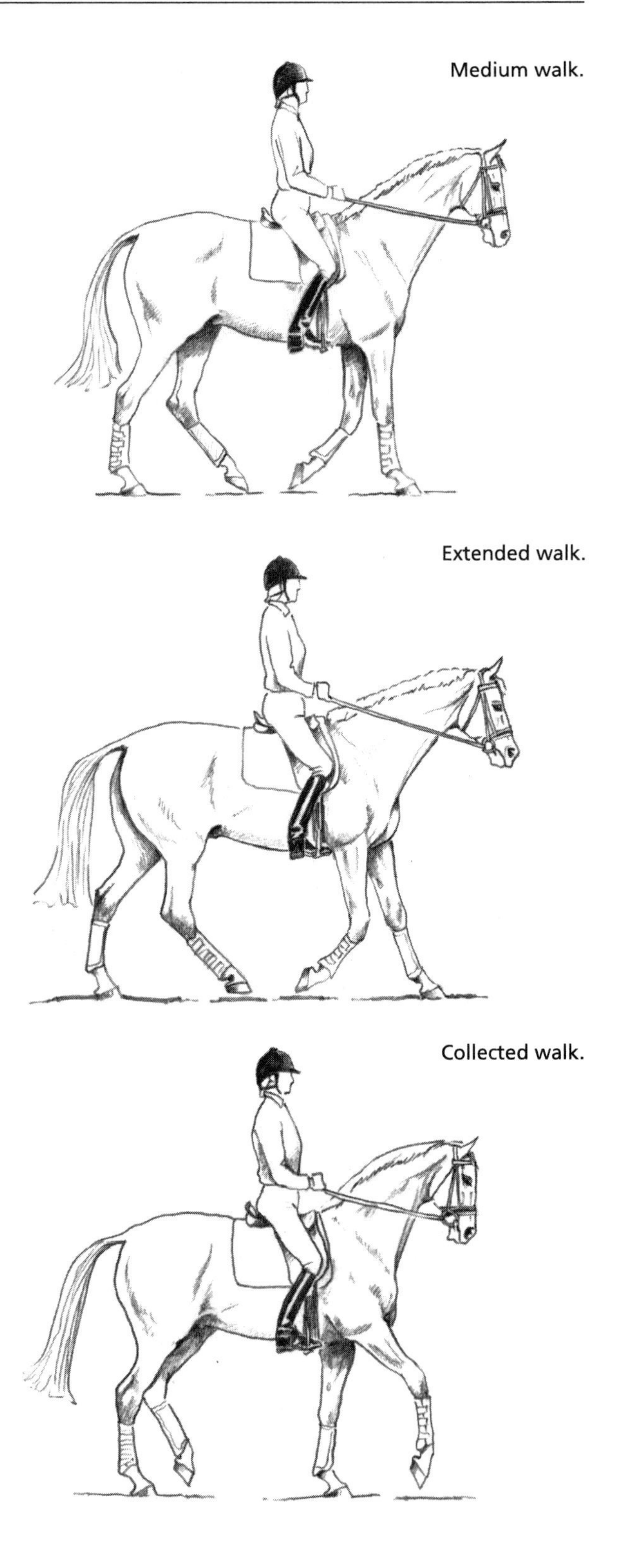

Medium walk.

Extended walk.

Collected walk.

Medium trot.

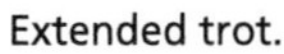
Extended trot.

Collected trot.

Medium gaits

These are gaits of moderate extension between working and extended.

Aims at all medium paces

- Longer strides than for working, but rounder and shorter than for extended.
- Unconstrained strides with rhythm and balance.
- To produce lively impulsion from the hindquarters.
- To keep the horse 'on the bit' (see page 88) with the head and neck slightly lower than in the working and collected paces. To extend the head more in front of the vertical than in the collected and working gaits.

Particular features

At the medium walk the hind feet should touch the ground in front of the footprints of the forefeet (overtracking). This is the walk at which the rider first works the young horse.

Extended gaits

In these the horse lengthens his strides to his utmost.

Aims at all extended paces

- The strides to be as long as possible while maintaining rhythm and balance.
- To produce lively impulsion from the hindquarters.
- The horse to remain calm, and light in the forehand.
- To keep the horse 'on the bit' with the head and neck lowered and lengthened so that the strides become longer, rather than higher.
- Not to make hurried strides.

Particular features

At the extended walk, overtracking should be more

Medium canter.

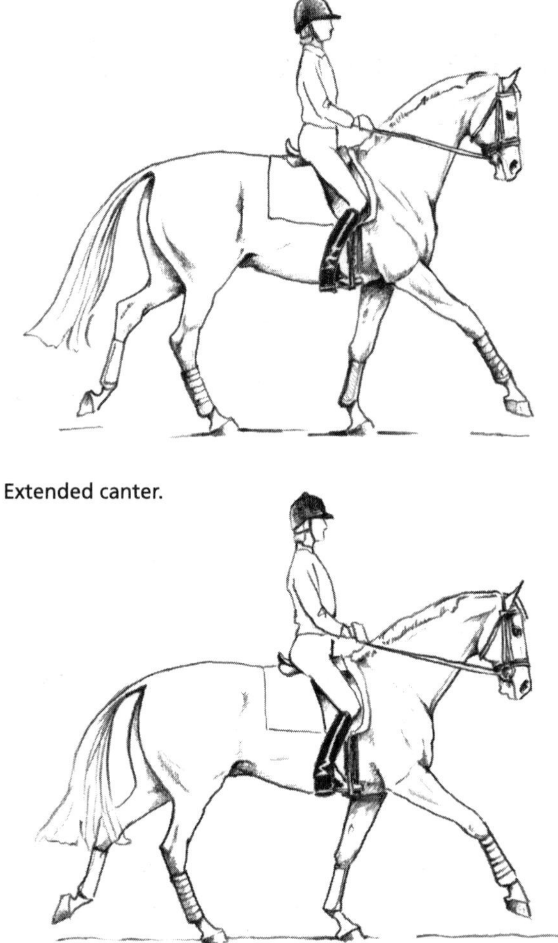

Extended canter.

Collected canter.

pronounced than in the medium and the rider should allow the horse to stretch out his head and neck but without losing contact with the mouth. At the extended trot there should be no flicking of the forelegs.

Collected gaits

In these the strides become shorter and higher and the horse is at his most manoeuvrable.

Aims at all collected paces

- To produce lively impulsion from the hindquarters, which are strongly engaged with the joints well bent. This should result in a lightening of the forehand and the shoulders becoming more free and mobile.
- To keep the horse 'on the bit' with his neck raised and arched so that there is an harmonious curve from the withers to the highest point – the poll. The head should be slightly in front of the vertical but may become more or less perpendicular when the rider uses his aids.
- The hind legs to be engaged.
- The quarters should be lowered.

Particular features

At the collected walk and trot the hind feet should touch the ground behind or in the footprints of the forefeet.

Free gaits

At these the horse is allowed complete freedom to lower and stretch his head and neck. He relaxes, but should remain active. The free walk is the most commonly used, especially for young horses, and as a reward for good work.

CHAPTER 8

THE INITIAL TRAINING OF THE RIDDEN HORSE

In the horse's natural state his instinctive defence is flight, and he only fights if provoked. The aim of early training is to overcome his fear, to earn his trust and obedience, and to turn the instinct of flight into a willingness to go forward at all times.

Efforts to do this should start from the time a foal is born, and if they are successful in the early stages they will greatly simplify the horse's subsequent training.

EARLY HANDLING

A foal should be handled from birth so that he learns to trust and respect humans and not to fear them. In the years before he is ridden he should be trained progressively to:

- Lead quietly.
- Be halter broken and tied up.
- Be groomed and have his feet picked out and trimmed.
- Accept the various items of tack used for breaking and riding.
- Become familiar with and learn not to fear a variety of strange sights and sounds.
- Obey the basic commands: e.g. 'walk on','whoa'.

INITIAL TRAINING

When the horse is three or four years old he should have developed sufficiently – physically and mentally – to undergo the concentrated and progressive training of being backed, ridden and learning the aids.

The stages of training

1. Leading in hand.
2. Lungeing.
3. Backing: i.e. teaching the horse to accept a rider on his back.
4. Being ridden on the lead and lunge.
5. Control by the rider.

Feeding during these stages must be carefully monitored. A young horse full of oats tends to be too spirited to understand and obey. It is vital to keep him sensible, which usually means limiting his feed (unless he is lazy and/or weak), and turning him out to grass whenever possible.

The length of training varies from horse to horse, depending largely on the horse's temperament, the extent and success of his initial handling, and the ability of the trainer.

As a rough guide, and assuming that the early handling of the foal and youngster has been satisfactory, a professional trainer usually takes four to six weeks to lead, lunge, back and quietly ride a young horse. This applies to training at a school where cost, and therefore time, is usually an important factor. It is essential for training not to be hurried. The horse should never be asked to carry out more than his condition or temperament warrant. Anyone wishing to train their own horse would be well advised to spend much longer on this early work. Extensive work on the lunge pays dividends later on, and up to twelve weeks can be spent on this stage.

Tack (see also page 76)

The following tack is needed:

- a lungeing cavesson;
- a snaffle bridle;
- a cotton or nylon webbing lunge rein;
- a roller and breast plate, or
- a saddle, preferably with numnah and breast plate;
- side-reins;
- boots, which should be worn on all four legs in all work;
- a neck strap, if a breast plate is not fitted.

The trainer needs a long lunge whip and should always wear gloves.

Fitting the tack

The items should be introduced one at a time, the horse being allowed to accept each new item quietly and calmly before another is tried.

To fit a lunge cavesson

This should be buckled firmly enough to avoid it being pulled around. The lead/lunge rein is normally fitted to the central ring of the cavesson.

To fit a bridle

The snaffle bit must fit the horse's mouth so that it is neither so narrow that it pinches, nor so wide that the joint falls far down in the horse's mouth. The mouthpiece should be quite thick and single-jointed. Some horses object to having a bridle fitted, however carefully this is done, and in such cases the bridle may be put on like a headcollar with the bit fastened to the off-side cheek piece only and allowed to hang down. The bit can then be put in the horse's mouth very gently before securing the near-side cheek piece firmly enough so that corners of the horse's mouth just wrinkle. If the bit is too low the horse can easily get his tongue over it, if too high it will be uncomfortable.

To fit a cavesson with a bridle – see page 76.

To fit a roller

Great care is necessary when first fitting a roller and later the saddle, as many horses are very disturbed by the restrictive feeling of the girth. One person is needed to hold the horse's head, also to help with adjustments on the horse's off-side if a third person is not available. The trainer stands on the near-side and places the roller, with the buckle end bent back over itself, very gently on the horse's back. The breast plate is attached to prevent the roller from slipping back, before the buckle end of the girth is gently slid down the horse's off-side, quietly brought under the horse, and drawn up to the retaining straps on the roller. It is attached very loosely at first, but if the horse is not upset it is gradually tightened by one or two holes at a time. It is advisable to move the horse forward a few steps between each tightening operation.

To fit a saddle

The same procedure is followed as for fitting the roller, including the attachment of the breast plate. Initially it is important for the girth to be only just tight enough to prevent the saddle from slipping; if too tight the horse will often buck against the pressure.

LEADING IN HAND

The foal

In most cases a horse is taught to lead in and out of his field or stable alongside his dam. To start with, the foal should be walked around his stable with a stable rubber around his neck, and a hand around his hindquarters. It is important to push rather than pull, helping to instil the willingness to go forward at an early age. Once he understands this, he may be led from a foal slip, but one hand should remain on or around the hindquarters, and it is this hand which deals with any arguments. The foal will soon learn that it is useless to resist and may then be led outside his stable, following his mother.

The young horse

If a young horse has missed this early training he can be taught to lead in a stable, preferably a large one, and it is best not to lead him outside until he is quiet and obedient on both reins.

A young horse should be led by a rein of about 3m (10ft) fastened to the central ring of a lunge cavesson. When the horse is used to a bridle, one may be fitted under the cavesson, but the lead rein should never be attached to the snaffle bit as this may spoil his mouth.

Assistance

In the early stages, unless the horse has been taught to move freely forward as a foal, it is advantageous for the trainer to have an assistant walking behind the horse. He can then send the horse forward if he tries to stop or run back.

Technique

The trainer should walk alongside, but not in front, of the horse's shoulder on the near-side, holding a whip in his left hand, which should be long enough to reach the hindquarters. If the horse draws back, or tries to stop, he can use his voice and the whip behind his back (see illustration below). Often the threat of the whip is sufficient to make the horse obey, but if necessary it can be applied gently and, if not effective, more strongly. Forward movement is of prime importance in the early and indeed all stages of training. If, however, the young horse tries to hurry or run on too much, repeated, rapid jerks on the front of the cavesson, together with the voice, can be used to slow him down or stop.

When the horse accepts being led on the near-side he should be taught to go equally well from the off-side. Before starting to lunge, the horse should obey the commands to 'walk on' and 'whoa'.

Use of the whip when the horse is reluctant to be led forward.

LUNGEING

Lungeing has a vital part to play in the training of the young horse, as long as it is carried out correctly. The next chapter describes in detail the technique of lungeing.

LONG REINING

In the past, long reining was widely practised as an alternative or supplement to lungeing, before backing was carried out. Although it enables a higher standard of training to be achieved, it requires special skills, and needs an experienced trainer if the young horse is not to be spoilt. The novice trainer should not experiment with long reining on a young horse, but should first learn the technique under the guidance of an expert, using an older horse as a guinea pig.

The stages

1. The horse is tacked up as for lungeing, with bridle, roller, cavesson, to which the lunge rein is attached on the central ring, and boots. The trainer carries a lunge whip and first settles the horse, lungeing him in the normal manner.

2. With the trainer holding the lunge rein and standing by the horse's inside shoulder, an assistant attaches a second lunge rein to the side ring on the outside of the cavesson, runs it back through the D on the roller and around the outside of the horse's hindquarters. This must be carried out with great care so that the horse will not be frightened by the feel of the rein. With a nervous horse, some people begin with the rein coming from the D over the horse's back, and progress from there to round the quarters.

3. The trainer is given the second (outside) rein but does not place any tension on this rein until the horse is calm and relaxed. The horse is asked to go forward in a circle around the trainer as on the lunge, with the inside rein acting as a normal lunge rein.

4. The inside rein is attached to the inside ring of the cavesson and run back through the D on the roller as with the outside rein. In work gradually more pressure is put on the outside rein to develop it as a controlling aid.

5. The horse is asked to change direction, at the walk, the previous outside rein becoming the inside one.

6. The reins are attached to the bit instead of the cavesson.

7. The horse is asked to go forward in straight lines and to turn corners with the trainer behind him.

Whether on a circle or a straight line, the horse can be asked to halt, move off and change his gait.

The time schedule for these stages depends on the temperament of the horse and on how advanced his training is. The vital factor is that the trainer only attempts the next stage if the horse is calm in the easier work.

Long reining is of value with a young horse to teach him the driving and 'steering' aids. It usually helps to establish a confident mouth, which makes control much easier once the horse is backed and ridden. Long reining is also very advantageous in advanced dressage work, as it is a useful aid to achieving collection and lateral work.

BACKING

Timing

The trainer must decide when a horse is ready to be backed, according to each individual case. It is generally not attempted until the horse is obedient, relaxed and working well on the lunge.

If the preparatory work has been carried out correctly, the horse should accept the rider quietly and with confidence. Conversely, a horse who reacts

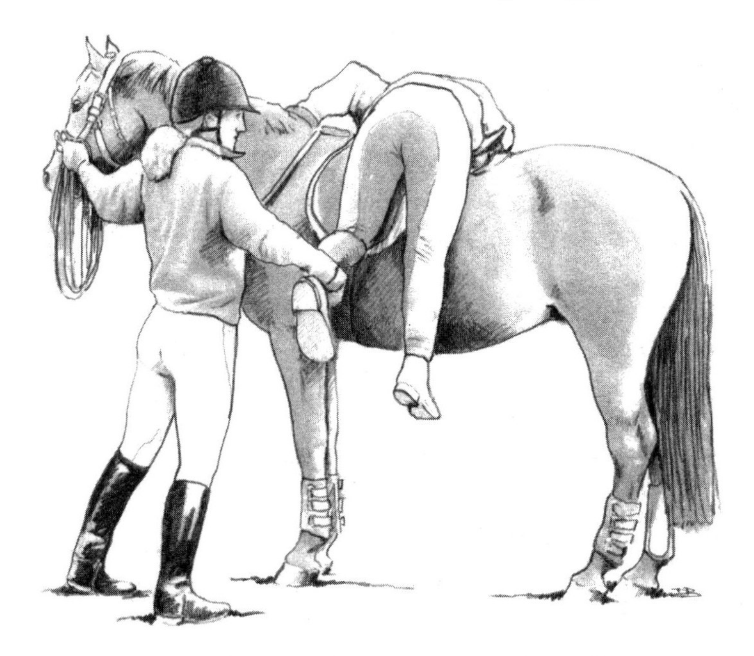

Legging up the rider to lean across the saddle.

violently to being backed has almost certainly been inadequately prepared or has had a previous bad experience.

Equipment

Backing is best carried out in an enclosed place, such as an indoor riding school or a small paddock – a stable is too confined and potentially unsafe. The horse should be fitted with a snaffle bridle under the cavesson, a breast plate, and a saddle, which most trainers prefer without stirrup leathers and irons.

Assistance

If possible, three people should be available: the trainer, who usually holds the horse; an assistant, who helps the rider to mount and dismount and to maintain his position on the saddle; and the rider. With an experienced trainer, however, backing can – and often has to be – achieved by two people. The trainer then both helps the rider to mount and holds the horse.

A useful aid is to place a straw bale by the horse for the rider to use as a mounting block and to help accustom the horse to seeing a human above him.

The stages

1. Before starting, the horse should be lunged to settle him. When the horse is relaxed and calm, the trainer stands at the horse's head, on the near-side, holding him by the lunge rein which is attached to the cavesson. The rider, also on the near-side, takes hold of the saddle, pats it, moves it gently about on the horse's back, jumps up and down a few times and then repeats this with one hand on the pommel and the other on the cantle. The whole procedure should then be repeated on the off-side.

2. If the horse remains calm, the trainer, or his assistant if he has one, can give the rider a leg up so that he can lean across the saddle (see above). This exercise can be repeated on the off-side. If the horse becomes upset, the trainer should comfort him and the rider can slide quietly to the ground. Whenever possible, the rider, whilst lying across the saddle, pats the horse on the opposite side. To reach this stage on the first day of backing is sufficient progress.

3. When the young horse accepts the rider leaning across the saddle from either side, he can be led

forward a few steps – but this position is tiring for the rider and cannot be held for long.

4. The rider can then start to move around a little on the saddle, both at the halt and as the horse is led forward. He can also slowly raise his head and shoulders.

5. As the horse becomes confident, the rider can put a leg over the saddle, taking care not to touch the horse's hindquarters, to sit astride. The top part of the rider's body is still kept low, near to the horse's neck. This is done at the halt, and when the horse remains calm he can be walked forward a few paces. The rider can then slowly raise his body so that the horse becomes used to him sitting upright.

At all times the rider and the trainer must be quick to reward the horse when he does well, by patting him on the neck and praising him.

Titbits should be avoided except as a reward at the end of the lesson.

RIDING ON THE LEAD AND LUNGE

When first ridden the horse is led forward quietly, with the rider sitting upright but relaxed. Control is in the hands of the person leading, who can play out the rein and move away until the horse is on the lunge circle. When the horse walks the circle calmly he can be asked to trot: at first when being led and then on the lunge. The rider starts in sitting trot with very little weight on the seat bones, but uses the rising trot as soon as his coming out of the saddle does not alarm the horse.

Equipment

Stirrups are used at the discretion of the rider; some prefer to use them from the start – but with caution, as they can get in the way and upset the horse by banging on his sides. The neck strap or breast plate is **always** worn and can be used by the rider to secure his position without interfering with the horse's mouth. The reins should be attached to the bit from the beginning, but only used in dire emergencies. Side-reins should **never** be fitted.

Introducing the aids

If the horse remains calm when being led around the school or paddock with the rider on his back, the aids can be introduced. The trainer, holding the lunge rein loosely, should encourage the horse to walk and halt, first in obedience to his voice and then to the rider's. The rider can then begin to introduce the rein and leg aids in conjunction with his voice. A schooling whip may be carried by the rider to reinforce when necessary (but with great care) the leg aids. However, depending on the temperament, manner and confidence of the horse, it may be wise to wait until the horse is working independently off the lunge before carrying and introducing a schooling whip.

Control by the rider

When the horse walks, trots, and halts calmly to the rider's aids, the lunge rein can be removed. To ensure a smooth changeover after detaching the rein, the trainer may continue to walk beside the horse, although leaving control to the rider, before moving away gradually.

The rider should concentrate on getting his horse to move forward calmly in answer to his aids, including the voice. When he wishes to make a turn he will have to rely more on the use of the reins as the voice will not mean anything. Moving a hand out boldly to the required side, but without any backward tension, he must still be riding the horse forward.

Quiet, clear commands and firm but kind handling should produce results, with the horse obeying the simple aids at walk and trot.

Cantering

There should be no hurry to teach the horse to canter with a rider. If started too early it can excite the young horse and may result in his losing his balance, even to the extent that the sequence of the pace and the length of stride is impaired.

To begin with, cantering should only be asked for on a straight line. On corners the horse can be allowed to fall back into the trot until repetition improves his balance and understanding of what is wanted. The rider merely takes up the correct position and gives encouragement until later when the more serious cantering lessons can start.

It is often easier for a young horse to canter if the rider adopts the basic position for jumping (page 42).

Standing still when mounted

For safety and discipline it is essential for the horse to remain still when mounted, both when the rider is legged up and when he uses the stirrup.

An assistant should hold the horse's head to ensure that he does not move when the rider is legged up and first learns to accept the rider mounting with a foot in the stirrup. These first lessons are best carried out at the end of a riding session so that the horse is relaxed and even a little tired.

As soon as the horse is not disturbed by this manner of mounting, the rider can mount using the stirrups at the beginning of a session, at first with an assistant holding the head, but after a few days without him. Then the rider must keep the horse immobile through use of the voice and, if necessary, the reins.

Acceptance of strange/unusual objects

An essential part of a young horse's training is to get him to accept strange sights and sounds without fear. Even when he is a foal, coloured poles can be placed on the ground at the entrance to his paddock and he can be encouraged to follow his dam over them. It is beneficial, too, to turn him out in a field from which traffic can be seen and heard.

Traffic

Motor vehicles are a serious hazard today and great care must be taken to train the young horse to accept them calmly. It is important to take every possible precaution to prevent him from being frightened by lorries or cars.

When riding outside for the first few times it is advisable to go with one or two trained quiet horses who can set an example and give confidence. At first the trained horse should be kept between the young horse and the traffic, and if he remains calm, the older horse can go in front of him, and eventually behind.

Shying

If a horse shies at an object, he should not be beaten or forced too close to it, but allowed to pass by at what he considers a safe distance and with his head bent away from it. If each time he passes the object causing concern, the rider can quietly ask him to go a little nearer, the horse should eventually overcome his fear to pass it without shying. In this way any argument can be avoided, and it is more likely that the cure will be permanent.

SUMMARY

When a young horse is able to walk, trot, and canter calmly under the control of his rider, and has had regular ridden exercise for two to three months, he should be sufficiently confident and physically fit to undertake the next stage of training.

CHAPTER

LUNGEING THE HORSE

Lungeing can be used throughout the training of the horse. As long as it is done well it improves the horse's physical coordination – developing his rhythm, balance, suppleness, willingness to go forward, and fitness; but probably even more important than this, it trains the horse's mind and can be a major influence on his mental outlook. Through lungeing, the horse can be taught to respect, trust and obey his trainer.

Major uses of lungeing

- The initial training of the young horse.
- Retraining spoilt horses.
- Exercising horses which are not being ridden.
- Settling and relaxing fresh or spirited horses before they are ridden.
- Advanced dressage work.
- To train the rider. (See Chapter 3.)

Lungeing is therefore a vital aspect of work with horses, but if the horse is to derive full benefit, it demands a trainer with considerable experience, skill and ability to anticipate the horse's movements.

EQUIPMENT

The lungeing area (see also page 35)

An area of flat ground large enough for a circle of at least 20m (22yds). It is an advantage if it is enclosed (sheep hurdles, poles, etc., can be used if an arena is not available), and if it is reasonably quiet so that the horse's attention can be maintained.

Tack

- A snaffle bridle, preferably with a simple snaffle bit which has quite a thick, single-jointed, smooth mouthpiece. Either a drop or cavesson noseband is worn (some people prefer to remove the noseband if a lungeing cavesson is fitted). If the reins are not removed they should never be attached to the stirrups or saddle; instead they can be twisted around under the neck and the throatlash put through one of the loops (see overleaf).

- A cavesson. This has a padded noseband with three metal rings attached at the front, and a cheek strap. The cavesson is fitted over the bridle and can be buckled either under the chin like a drop noseband, or above the bit like a cavesson noseband. The lunge rein is fastened to the central swivel ring on the noseband. The noseband and cheek strap should be tightened sufficiently to avoid the cheek strap being pulled round to rub the horse's outside eye.

- A lunge rein of about 10m (33ft) long, made of natural fibre or synthetic webbing, with a large loop at one end and a swivel joint attached to a buckle or spring clip at the other.

- Side-reins, which should be about 2m (6 ft) long,

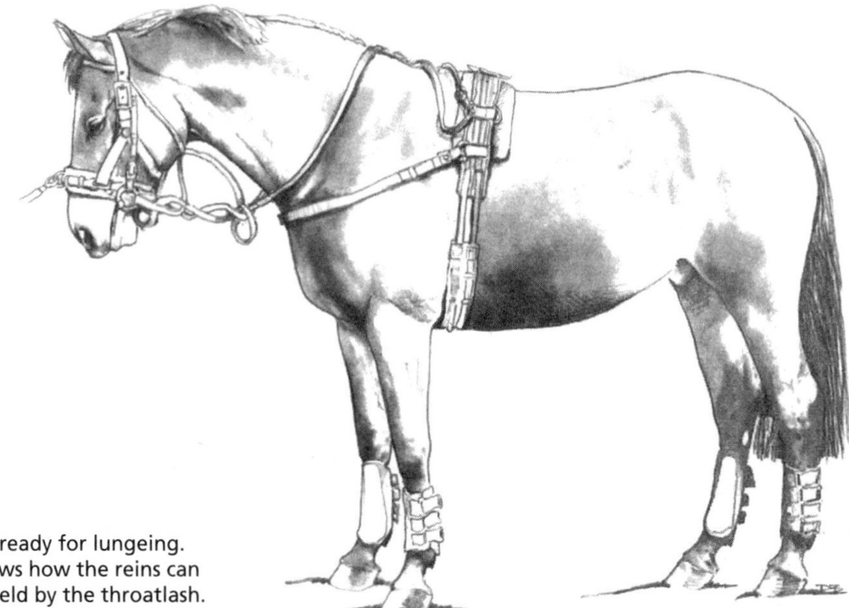

Horse tacked up ready for lungeing. The drawing shows how the reins can be twisted and held by the throatlash.

with a clip at one end and a buckle at the other. There should be a large number of holes at the buckle end so that there is scope for varying the length.

- A roller with rings on either side to which the side-reins can be attached.
- A breast plate to stop the roller or saddle slipping back.
- A saddle, possibly with numnah.
- Boots that are worn on all four legs to prevent damage to them from knocks.
- A lungeing whip with a thong which is long enough to reach the horse.

LUNGEING TECHNIQUE

The trainer

The trainer should wear **gloves** when lungeing so that if the rein is pulled quickly through his hands it will not burn them. He should also wear a hat.

He should **never** wear spurs as these can trip him over.

The trainer who stands correctly will be more efficient and able to react quickly to control the horse who suddenly pulls or turns. In the correct stance:

- The upper body is erect.
- The upper arms hang down with the forearms roughly at right angles to the body.
- The legs are slightly apart.
- Body language is an important aid in the control of the horse on the lunge.

The lunge rein

This should be held in the hand to which the horse is moving and the whip in the other. The end of the rein is looped so that it can be played out without tangling, and the loops are held in whichever hand the trainer finds it easier to handle the rein efficiently and without getting it tangled.

The lunger's position

The trainer stands at an angle of about 35° to 40° to the horse's forehand, with the horse's head just in front of his leading shoulder and himself in line with the horse's hips. He should concentrate on the movement in the horse's hindquarters rather than the forehand, aiming to drive the horse in a circle around him. Control over the hindquarters is vital if the trainer is to prevent the horse stopping or turning. The aim should be for the horse, the whip and the rein to form a triangle (see illustration below).

The horse should describe a true circle, so the trainer aims to stand on one spot, pivoting around one heel. With the young horse, however, in order to remain in control it might be necessary for the trainer to shorten the rein, move closer to the horse and walk in a small circle. For the horse, though, small circles are a strain: therefore a young horse should never be asked to describe a circle of less than 20m diameter. Only fit, trained horses can be asked to lunge in a smaller circle.

The lungeing aids

The aim is for these to simulate the aids used when riding. The lunge rein is equivalent to the reins; the whip to the legs, and the voice is used in conjunction with both these aids.

The rein should be used by the trainer to maintain a light, consistent contact with the horse, and the aids should be applied with quick movements of the fingers or, if the horse starts to lean on the rein, by giving and restraining, but not by pulling against him.

The whip is used as an aid; the horse should not fear it, but rather he should respect it as he would a schooling whip when being ridden. The horse should therefore be familiarised with it before lungeing and should learn to accept the whip being rubbed along his side and hindquarters.

During lungeing the whip can be applied if needed to make the horse move forward or to increase the activity of the hindquarters. It should be flicked just above the hind fetlocks – but quietly; the trainer should not lurch forward and loosen the rein. Normally the threat of the whip with a swing or a crack is sufficient. The whip is also used to keep the horse out on the circle. If he starts to cut corners or to fall in, it can be pointed and, if

Route of horse and trainer, when the horse lengthens his stride or jumps on the lunge.

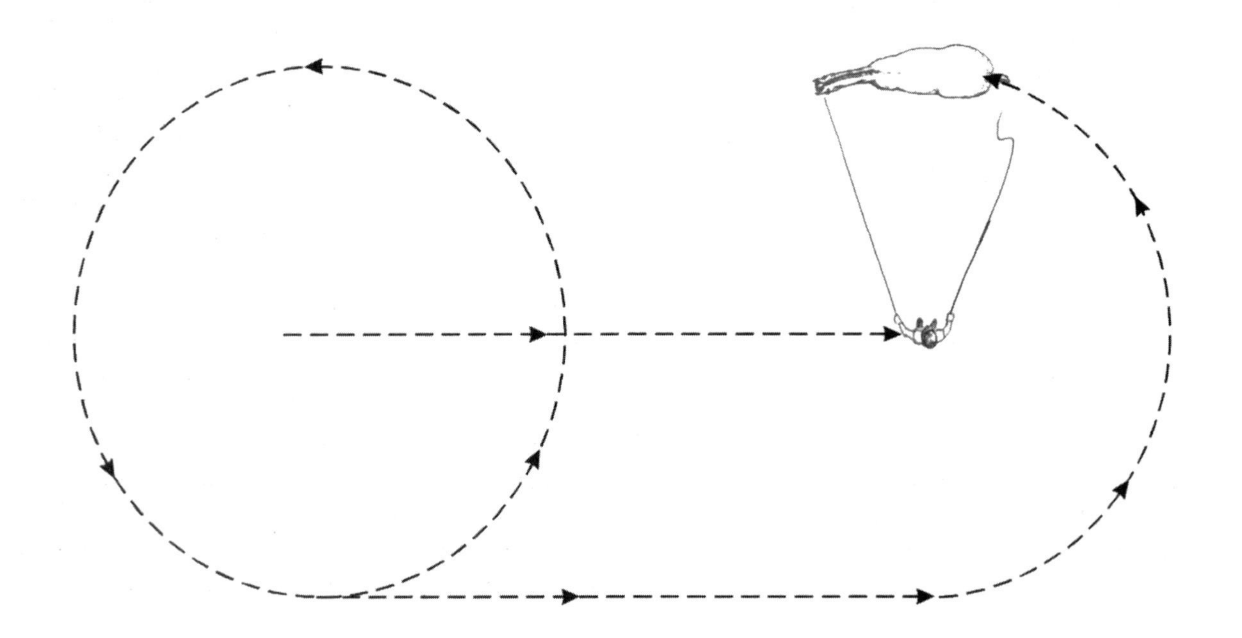

necessary, flicked in the direction of his shoulder.

The voice is the aid used most frequently, minimising the use of the whip to make the horse go forward and use of the rein to make him slow down. It is also used to soothe and calm the horse and to help him establish a rhythm to his gaits. The effectiveness of the voice is achieved at first in conjunction with the rein and whip aids so that the horse learns that a sharp quick command 'walk on', 'trot', 'canter', means to move forward, and if low and drawn-out 'whoa', 'wa-alk', 'ter-rot', to reduce the pace.

The tone of the voice is more important than the actual words used. Lifting the tone of the voice to increase pace and lowering it to decrease pace is usually very effective.

The work on the lunge

It is advisable to start on the rein which the horse finds the easier (usually the left) although he should be worked equally on both reins.

The time spent on the lunge will depend largely on his stage of training, his fitness, and the type of work on the lunge – he could walk for a long time but canter for considerably less. As a general rule, five to ten minutes on each rein is sufficient for a green or unfit horse, and as he gets stronger and more balanced this can be gradually increased to a lesson of about ten to fifteen minutes on each rein.

The horse must **never** be overworked: otherwise he will lose his enthusiasm and/or might be physically strained.

The novice horse

As soon as a horse is accustomed to wearing a bridle and cavesson, being led from both sides, and has learned to obey the voice aids to walk on and stand still, then he can be lunged.

For the first lesson he should wear the same tack in which he was led – just a snaffle bridle, cavesson and boots. The lunge rein is attached to the central ring on the cavesson.

Assistance

It is advisable for all but the most experienced trainers to use an assistant during these first lessons. The assistant can then lead the horse from the inside of the circle with the lunge rein running through his hands to the trainer in the centre. Once the horse has understood that he is supposed to move around in a circle, the assistant can move closer and closer to the trainer, and if the horse stays out, quietly walk out of the way. The same process should be repeated on the other rein.

It can be dangerous for the assistant to lead the horse from the outside.

The halt

When the horse describes a true circle, he must be taught to halt and walk on when commanded. When being led the horse should have learned that 'whoa' and vibrations on the rein mean 'stop'. These same aids should be applied on the lunge, taking care to control the hindquarters with the whip to prevent the horse from turning in towards the trainer. At first this may require the aid of the assistant.

The horse should halt on the track of the circle (some trainers do ask him to walk in towards them, but this can be detrimental since it encourages the horse to turn in of his own volition). He should not be asked to remain immobile for more than a few seconds. The trainer should then either ask him to walk on again or go out to him (keeping his whip behind him) to reward with pats, talking and occasional tit-bits.

If the horse does not halt, remember that it may not be through disobedience, but misunderstanding, so be patient. If he persists, work him close to a high ledge or wall (that is unjumpable). If he does not listen to the command to halt/whoa, keep him between the whip and rein to stop him turning in or running down the wall, and direct him towards the wall/high hedge, repeating the command. He will be forced to stop. This method of stopping can, however, cause some horses to panic and rush away from the influence of both the wall

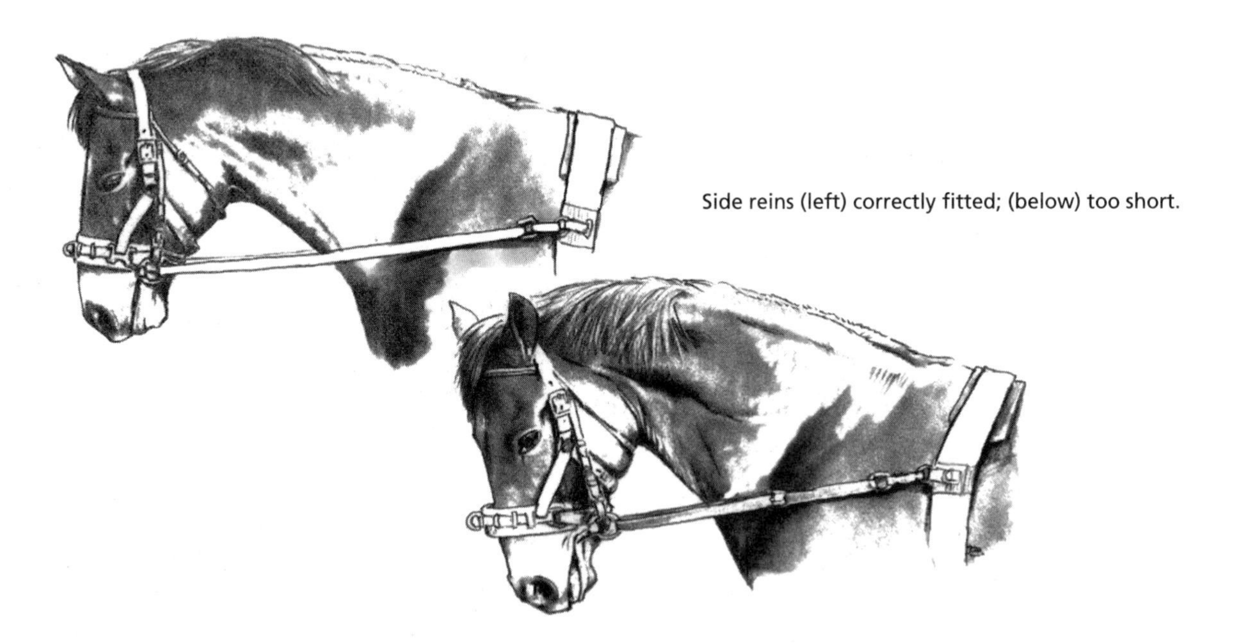

Side reins (left) correctly fitted; (below) too short.

and the trainer, so needs to be used with caution. When he does stop, make much of him.

The schedule

There can be no time schedule for the lessons below. The horse should master each one in turn, and should be able to remain calm, relaxed and obedient, before progressing to the next. The early lessons should be performed without side-reins at a free walk and at a working trot. It is best not to canter until the horse is stronger, but if fresh he can be allowed to canter until he settles sufficiently to pay attention.

The stages

Lungeing with a roller. The roller is fitted as on page 70, and the horse is lunged with it in place. The horse has to learn to relax and move freely with this restriction around his back and belly.

Lungeing with a saddle. When the horse is relaxed with a roller it can be replaced by a saddle. At first the stirrups should be removed. In a later lesson they can be run up, and finally before he is backed can be allowed to hang free for a short time so that the horse gets used to being touched where the rider's legs will be.

Lungeing with side-reins. These are attached to either the roller or the saddle a little above half way up the horse's side. To prevent them slipping down, the rings on the roller are preferable attachments. Before attaching them to the bit, the side-reins are made as long as possible and of equal length, then crossed over at the withers and attached to the Ds on the saddle or roller. The horse is then lunged for a few minutes on both reins to supple up and relax.

The side-reins are then unclipped, and most trainers then attach them directly on to the bit, but some recommend attaching them to the side rings on the cavesson for the first lessons. The horse is then lunged with the side-reins so loose that he cannot feel their effect.

When he works calmly and rhythmically (it might be during that lesson or two or three later), the side-reins can be shortened, but making sure that they both remain of an equal length.

The side-reins should be adjusted to such a length that the horse makes contact with them when he engages his hindquarters, rounds his back and lowers his head. The aim is that as the horse has made the contact himself he will not fear it but will soon start to seek it and to chew gently at the bit.

The side-reins should not be used to pull the horse's head into a particular position, nor should they be so tight that his head comes behind the vertical (see illustration opposite). The horse's state of balance and way of going must always dictate their length. It is also dangerous for the horse to walk much with the side-reins attached, as they restrict the natural movement of his head and make it more difficult to maintain the correct rhythm of the pace.

As the horse's balance improves he can bring his hind legs further underneath him, his outline becomes shorter and rounder, and the side-reins slacken. This is the time to shorten the side-reins, but never so much that the horse stiffens and resists against them.

Some trainers only use the side-reins for a brief period when familiarising the horse with the contact of the bit, before backing. They prefer to give the horse the freedom both to find his own balance and to stretch forward and down. This also avoids the danger of the horse resisting the contact by either hollowing his back and raising his head (above the bit) or getting over-bent and falling behind the contact (behind the bit).

Straightness on the lunge

Young horses are not straight (see page 87) but lunge work with side-reins helps to reduce crookedness. This is not achieved by shortening the inside rein, which only swings the hindquarters to the outside, throwing the weight on to the inside shoulder and tending to make him want to bend to the outside and resist.
If the side-reins are kept at the same length, when the horse places his inside hind leg well under him, which he must do to turn in a circle, his weight will be transferred diagonally towards the outside shoulder. To maintain his balance he will turn his head and neck to the inside. The pressure on the outside rein becomes stronger and the mouth becomes moist on that side, whereas the inside rein becomes looser.

Variations of gait and gaits

The horse can be encouraged to extend the length of his trot stride to do some medium trot, and this is easiest for him if he is driven out of the circle on to a straight line and then returned into a circle in a different place, when he can be brought back again into the working trot. (See illustration on page 78.) The canter is introduced when the horse can trot with rhythm, has a willingness to go forward, and moves with a supple swinging back. Its introduction should be a gradual process, the trainer asking at first for just a few strides on both reins. It is usually advisable to remove the side-reins for early lessons at the canter.

It is important for the trainer to recognise if faults are occurring at any of the gaits (i.e. four-time canter). He should aim to improve the horse's gaits all the time, and to do this must have a clear picture of what is correct. (See Chapter 7.)

Backing

A horse which is calm when wearing a saddle and accepts the bit happily at the trot can be backed, but the more time spent on the lunge, the easier it will be for the rider to train the horse. It is, however, advisable for the horse to learn to accept the weight of the rider before he gets too fit and strong. Many trainers therefore back him while continuing with training on the lunge: i.e. lunge him for fifteen to twenty minutes before he is ridden or alternate days of lungeing with days of riding.

LUNGEING OVER OBSTACLES

Lungeing over poles

This helps to give variety to the work and encourages the young horse to lower his head, round his back and flex his joints. The side-reins are always removed for this work and for all jumping. The horse is first led over the pole, and if he remains relaxed is then lunged at the walk and trot on a circle which is just short of the pole. When he relaxes he can be driven out of the circle and over the pole.

When lungeing over obstacles the trainer must ensure that:

- The horse is presented straight at the pole and does not approach it at an acute angle which would encourage him to run out. This means that the trainer will have to move at right angles to the pole and the horse will no longer describe a circle (see illustration on page 78).
- The horse is given as much freedom as possible over the pole and is not restricted by the lunge rein from lowering his head.
- The horse is driven from behind. The trainer should never get in front of him.
- The work is done in equal amounts on both reins.
- The trainer allows the horse to take a number of straight strides upon landing and is not pulled straight back into a circle.

When the horse walks and trots in a relaxed manner over this single pole in both directions, the exercise can be extended. Poles over which he can be lunged can be scattered around the school or laid in a series either in a straight line or round in a circle. They should be about 1.2–1.4m (4ft-4ft 6in.) apart. (See also page 124.) It is important for them to remain at the correct distance, and if a pole is displaced by the horse the poles should not be attempted again until correctly positioned. Heavy poles help to prevent this occurrence.

Lungeing over raised poles

When the horse trots over the poles in a relaxed manner, maintaining his rhythm and lowering his head, raised poles on blocks can be introduced. The same techniques are used as for poles on the ground (i.e. leading over, using single ones first and progressing to a series).

Well-prepared obstacle for lungeing.

Lungeing over a jump

Ideally the wing stands of the fence should be low. A pole should be leant against the inside jump stand to prevent the lunge rein being fouled and to act as a wing (see below). With the poles on the ground the horse is led over the jump.

The horse is then lunged over the jump with the poles on the ground. When he does this calmly and without rushing, the end of the pole nearest to the trainer can be raised. When the horse is happy trotting over this, another pole can be added to make a cross bar, and after this a third bar laid along the top, and later a fourth bar to make a parallel.

It is important to make the jumping fun for the horse, and so the progress should be gradual. He should not be asked too much nor should the lessons be too long.

MORE ADVANCED WORK ON THE LUNGE

The main purposes of lungeing more advanced horses are:

- As a means of loosening up horses which, in their

preliminary work, stiffen against the weight of the rider.

- As a visual aid to the trainer, who can study from the ground whether his horse is going straight, has sufficient impulsion and suppleness, and that the gaits are true.
- As an aid to collection at the trot and canter. The horse can be gradually brought on to smaller and smaller circles (but never so small that he loses his rhythm or his back stops swinging), while the trainer asks for as much impulsion as possible. Then while maintaining this collection the horse is allowed to go back on to a larger circle.
- As an aid to extension at the trot. The horse can be brought into a collected trot, then driven out of the circle on to a straight line, in the same manner as medium trot was asked for in variations of gait on page 67.
- Teaching piaffe (and very occasionally passage) in hand. This work is carried out on straight lines and is described on pages 116–17.

CHAPTER 10

TRAINING PRINCIPLES FOR RIDDEN WORK

A horse which has completed the training covered in Chapter 8, 'The Initial Training of the Horse', should be moving freely forward, calmly and confidently beginning to understand the basic aids of the rider. In order for the horse to develop and improve, his trainer/rider needs to understand the essential training principles of rhythm, balance, impulsion, suppleness, straightness and acceptance of the bit – all of which are set out in this chapter.

The basic training of the horse

- Stimulates his willingness to go forward.
- Develops his natural abilities.
- Strengthens his physique.
- Makes him more supple and gymnastic.
- Increases his stamina.
- Gives the rider more control.

GENERAL PRINCIPLES

The following are important:

- **Avoidance of short cuts.** Training requires time, effort and patience. Short cuts, such as the use of gadgets, should be avoided as these develop resistances and create their own problems.
- **Rate of progress.** Training cannot be conducted to a time-scale; it must be dependent on the progress made. The rate of progress will vary according to the ability and temperament of the horse and the rider. Although the trainer plans a programme for progressive training, it must be sufficiently flexible to suit the individual characteristics of the horse being trained.
- **Use of reward and punishment.** The following system of training uses rewards and punishments, but no force, to teach the acceptance of the aids and obedience to the rider. The amount of reward and punishment will vary according to the character of the horse. Hot-blooded, high-spirited horses usually need more rewards than lazy horses, who may benefit from occasional reprimands. The trainer must analyse the character of his horse and apply the appropriate discipline. In all cases persuasion is recommended as being more effective than coercion. A frightened horse is too tense to learn. The aim must be willing cooperation obtained by rational and tactful methods, but at the same time there must never be any doubt as to who is in command; if authority and respect are lost, training stops.

THE TRAINER/RIDER

Since it is the rider who trains the horse it will be assumed throughout this chapter that the trainer is the rider.

Qualities of a good trainer

- Ability to make the horse understand. If the horse does not obey, the trainer must consider whether his instructions were understood. Before blaming the horse he should examine his aids and methods.

  NB If a good basic position has been established by the trainer the aids can be given more clearly.

- An understanding of the general nature of a horse and an ability to adapt his approach according to the temperament and individual characteristics of the horse he is training.
- Patience and persistence.
- Temper must always be controlled.
- An air of calm authority when with the horse: ensuring that all movements are quiet and deliberate.
- Tolerance of playful high spirits in a young horse, but firmness in the face of wilful disobedience.
- A good sense of rhythm.
- A sufficient knowledge of horsemastership in order to ensure that his horse is being well cared for and suitably fed.

EQUIPMENT

This should include:

- A snaffle bridle with a drop, flash or cavesson noseband.
- A long schooling whip which can be used to reinforce leg aids.
- Brushing boots to be worn on all four legs.
- An enclosed area, preferably on good going, for work on the flat.

OBJECTIVES OF TRAINING

The following objectives are the basis of all training. It is difficult to place them in order of priority because they are inter-related, with improvements to one being dependent upon – and having repercussions on – other objectives. Also, as methods of achieving them overlap, several may be worked on simultaneously. As each horse has different strengths and weaknesses the importance of work on a particular objective will vary. The seven objectives are:

1. Controlled forward impulsion.
2. Rhythm and balance.
3. Suppleness.
4. Straightness.
5. Acceptance of the bit.
6. Submission.
7. Development of the gaits.

Controlled forward impulsion

'Impulsion is a tendency to move forward with elasticity, originating from the haunches, flowing into a swinging back and ending in the mouth' (Colonel Handler). It is **contained energy** created by the activity of the hindquarters and should be instantly ready for the rider to call on. The consequent willingness and ability of the horse to go forward is the foundation of all work. If impulsion is lost it should be recreated before other movements are attempted.

NB Impulsion is **not** speed. A horse which has impulsion should be able to establish a slower rhythm to his gaits.

To develop impulsion

The first step is to achieve the basis of impulsion – **the willingness to go forward.** Until the horse goes forward to the aids it will be difficult to control him (a stationary horse cannot be steered and a lazy/slow one only with difficulty).

The horse must therefore be made responsive to the leg – to be in front of the leg. Leg aids can, if necessary, be supported by the voice and taps with the whip. As the training progresses and the horse gains his rhythm and balance, more forward momentum can be created and the seat aids can be brought into action. This forward momentum, instead of producing more speed, can be partly contained within the horse (impulsion). The driving aids, rather than simply making him go forward can – if the rider's hands restrain but allow (half-halt)– result in the horse's hindquarters becoming more engaged and active. This gives the horse the power to go forward as soon as he is asked.

In creating this forward impulsion it is important for it not to be associated with speed. He should never be asked to go forward so much that he begins to lose balance and goes faster, nor should so much impulsion be created that the rider cannot control it, for then the tendency is to pull the reins backwards, which destroys the impulsion and creates resistance.

Rhythm and balance

Rhythm is the regular recurrence of a given time interval between one footfall and the next in any of the paces. Each pace has its own rhythm. The walk is four-time (1-2-3-4), the trot is two-time (1-2, 1-2), and the canter three-time (1-2-3).

NB Tempo should be distinguished from rhythm. It is the SPEED of the rhythm: the time it takes for a sequence of the footfalls to occur. **Cadence** is when a pace has pronounced rhythm,which gives it an appearance of 'lift' and greater presence. (See 'Improvement of the gaits', page 90.)

Importance of rhythm

As in so many other spheres of activity (athletics, ballet, etc.) rhythm is vital to make best use of ability. When a horse has rhythm he is also likely to be balanced and will find it easier to remain calm and relaxed. Many trainers believe that rhythm is the clearest and easiest primary objective. When it is achieved the horse should be balanced, calm and relaxed.

To develop rhythm

The aim is to get a horse to maintain the rhythm of a particular pace on circles, straight lines and through corners. To do this he must be balanced.

When a horse is moving freely in his paddock he has natural balance, but when he starts to be ridden the weight of the rider puts him on his forehand. If he maintains his natural balance this will make it difficult to keep a rhythm. The hind legs will tend to push the weight rather than lift it, which will usually make the gaits flat, heavy and irregular. To be balanced, in a rhythm when carrying a rider, the horse has to engage his hind legs, bringing them further underneath his and the rider's body. To achieve this, the rider applies short but repeated aids with legs, and later with the seat, asking the horse to go forward to a restraining but allowing hand (half-halts). At the same time the rider must think of the rhythm of the gait.

Suppleness

A horse must be supple in order to be a comfortable ride and to make best use of his physique. The aim is a suppleness which allows the relaxed coordination of every muscle and joint. Tension is the major restriction on such an aim – for whether it is caused by excitement, apprehension, or resistance, it not only reduces concentration but it also inhibits freedom of movement. To be supple the horse should be calm and relaxed. The most common area of tension is the back – for the horse naturally tends to stiffen and become rigid under the weight of the rider. This makes it difficult for the rider to sit in the saddle, to apply his seat aids and to feel the actions of the horse, and for the aids to come 'through'. (See 'Submission', page 90.)

The horse's back muscles should be supple and

should 'swing' so that the muscles behind the saddle move in unison with the horse's legs to provide an elastic connection, and so coordinate the hindquarters and the forehand. At the walk, sitting trot and canter, the trainer must be supple enough not to impede the horizontal and vertical movement in the horse's back.

To develop suppleness

The horse has to be suppled both laterally and longitudinally.

To supple him laterally he must learn to bend round the rider's inside leg. This is achieved by working through circles, loops and serpentines, and later, in lateral work, particularly shoulder-in. He must not be allowed to increase the weight on the inside rein and must be encouraged to engage the inside hind leg. Care must be taken that the amount of bend asked for is equal on both reins.

To supple him longitudinally means that:

- He brings his hind legs more underneath his body.
- He learns to lift and swing his back.
- He makes his top line rounder by lengthening the muscles along his back and neck.

This is most easily done on large circles. The horse is ridden from the inside leg into the outside rein and encouraged with half-halts to work in a rounder manner. The horse should soon start to lower his head, going forward to the hand, with the rider encouraging greater engagement of the hindquarters. The rider must allow this 'working down' and not restrict the swinging back muscles with his seat or block with his reins. The rhythm and impulsion must be maintained otherwise the horse will go on to his forehand and the whole object of the exercise will be lost.

Other important suppling exercises are: frequent well-executed transitions, encouragement of the willingness to go forward, use of trotting poles and small fences and, later, lateral work.

Straightness

The horse is straight when the hind legs follow the tracks of the forelegs, which means when moving on straight lines he will be straight and on curved lines slightly bent from nose to tail along the line of the curve. There should not be any greater bend in the neck than in the rest of the body.

To make the horse straight

The untrained horse is rarely straight and the rider will feel that the horse accepts the rein contact more readily on one side than on the other. The hind leg will bend more on the hollow side and will not truly follow the track of the corresponding foreleg. Therefore, the shorter muscles on the hollow side have to be lengthened gradually, to avoid strain and stress. Forcible bending of the neck produces tension, resistance and tilting of the head. It is important to avoid concentrating entirely on the forehand, as the hind leg which is slightly left behind must be encouraged to come forward and under the body.

It is difficult to make a horse truly straight until he is capable of performing the best of all straightening exercises – the shoulder-in. By this stage, too, the hindquarters will be more engaged and the shoulders easier to control: therefore not too much emphasis should be placed on straightening the young horse. The following is excellent preliminary work.

If the horse is stiff to the right and hollow to the left he will be slightly bent in his whole body around the rider's left leg and may tend to bend his neck too much to that side and will drop the inside rein. With such a horse the trainer begins his schooling sessions riding on the left rein (which is the easier for the horse) and concentrates at first in preventing him from bending his neck too much to the left. Contact with the left rein is maintained while using short, gentle taking-and-giving actions with the right rein to reduce the excess bend in the neck. At the same time the trainer uses his leg (and seat) aids to push the horse forward into the hand to obtain an even and momentarily stronger contact. (A very green horse will rarely take enough contact to do this.) It is important – as with all work – for the use of the seat and leg aids and the maintenance of the will to go forward to be kept uppermost in the mind during these straightening exercises. An excess of rein aids leads to resistance and the horse dropping behind the aids.

After several circuits the rider should change the bend and repeat the same lesson on the more difficult rein for the horse. On this rein the rider asks for more bend by riding from the inside leg into a still, outside rein, using taking-and-giving aids with the inside rein. Equal amounts of work should be done on both reins.

The aids for correcting a stiffness to the right should be reversed if the horse is stiff to the left.

NB The rider should gradually experience a more even feel on the reins and have less difficulty in correcting the bend in the neck, but it is a slow process, as muscles must develop to enable the horse to get straighter.

The problem of one-sided stiffness has to be dealt with throughout the training of most horses. At times the feel on both reins may be the same, even then the following day slight stiffness on one side may be felt.

Acceptance of the bit

The horse accepts the bit when he maintains a light, elastic rein contact with the rider without resistance and with submission throughout his body. When jumping, riding out, or in early stages of training, he may accept the bit without fulfilling the conditions necessary to be 'on the bit'.

To **accept the bit**, the horse should be:

- Worked so that he develops a constant willingness and ability to go forward (impulsion).
- Trained so that he is straight and accepts the same contact on either side of his mouth.
- Encouraged to 'seek the bit' from quite an early stage of his education. The trainer should, as soon as possible, take a light but positive and continuous contact with the bit through the reins. By keeping the horse calm and in rhythm, using an 'asking' leg and 'allowing' hand, but without losing contact, the rider should soon induce the horse to move forward on to the bit. The horse can be allowed to carry his head in a natural position as long as the rider follows the mouth to maintain a light contact, with a forward, not pulling, tension through the reins. The rider should, in effect say: 'this is my hand and you must accept it', so the horse finds that the hand is acceptable and there is no point in resisting it.

A horse is **on the bit** if:

- The hocks are correctly placed.
- The neck is more or less raised and arched, according to the stage of training and the extension or collection of the pace.
- He accepts the bit without resistance, with a light and soft contact, a relaxed jaw, and submission throughout his body.
- The head remains steady and, as a rule, slightly in front of the vertical.
- A supple poll is the highest point of the neck.

The rein contact should not be hard and solid, nor should it be so light that it is like holding a thread. A correct contact means a consistent elastic easy tension that comes from a forward tendency originating in the hindquarters and passes 'through' a relaxed and swinging back, the neck and so to the mouth, where it is accepted evenly on both sides. Such a contact is only possible when the horse is in balance, carrying himself and not relying on support from the reins. Balance and contact are therefore complimentary – the better the balance, the better the contact, and vice versa.

The horse uses his head and neck to balance himself, so the trainer should never use the reins to place the head in a particular position. A horse will carry his

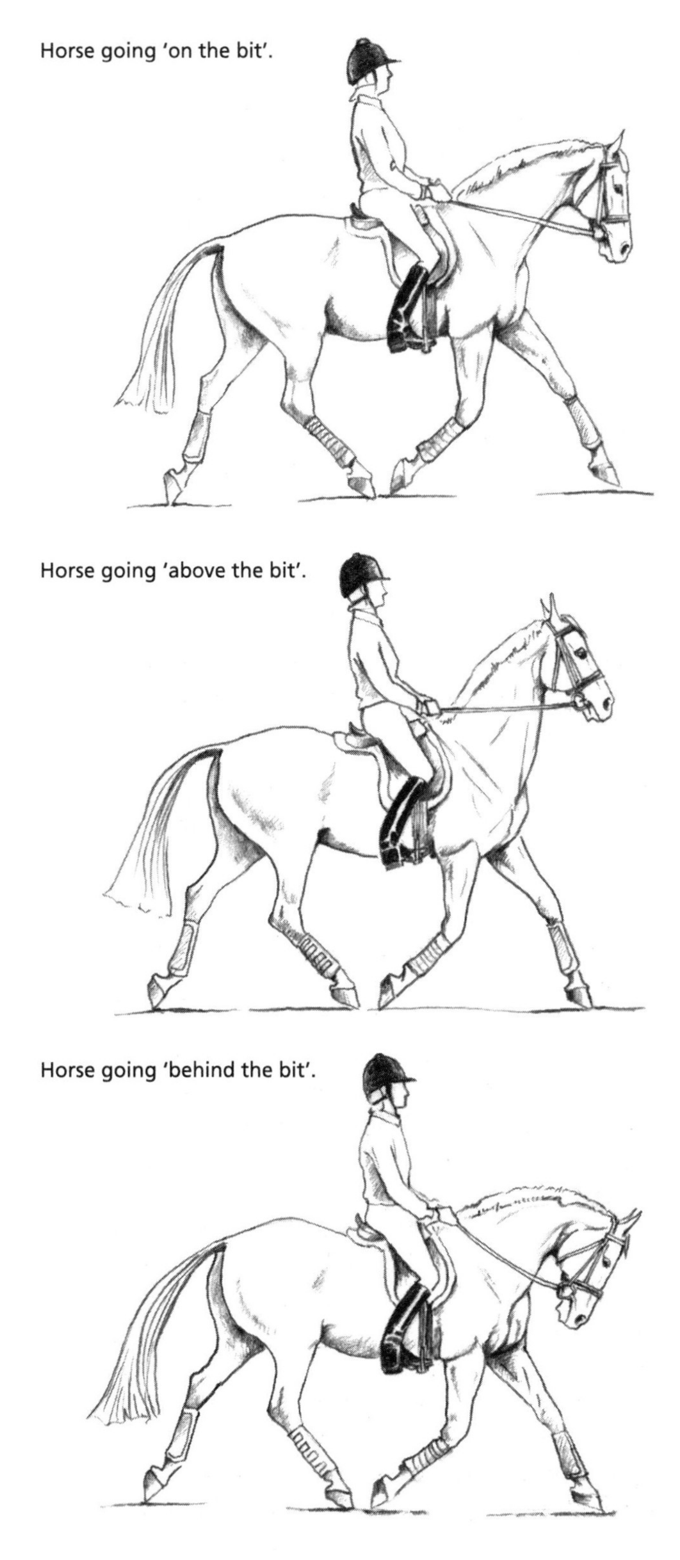

Horse going 'on the bit'.

Horse going 'above the bit'.

Horse going 'behind the bit'.

head in accord with his conformation, the stage of training he has reached, the flexibility of all his joints and the activity on his hindquarters.

If the horse pulls on the reins in an effort to go faster, the trainer, with many downward transitions and repeated taking-and-giving actions of the reins, should make him accept a balance and rhythm on a lighter contact.

If the horse is **above the bit** (see left) his head is held high, the angle of the head is too far in front of the vertical and his back becomes hollow. Such a horse should be given exercises to develop a stronger and more rounded back. (See 'To develop suppleness', page 87.) He is usually best worked at the rising trot, or in bad cases, at the walk. The rein contact should be particularly sympathetic, the rider trying to feel with his hand, encouraging the horse to bend his poll, relax his lower jaw and stop resisting the contact. The horse should be ridden forward to a rein contact and asked to engage his hindquarters which will encourage him to round his back and lower his head. This is especially effective when working on a circle when the trainer can ride positively to the outside rein asking intermittently with an open inside rein for the bend and allowing as soon as there is any submission to the outside rein. The reins should not be used to pull the head down, as this blocks the engagement of the hindquarters and creates resistance.

If the horse is **behind the bit** (see left) he does not accept the rein contact, the front of the face is behind the vertical, and the poll is no longer the highest point of the neck. This can be due to the rider's hands being too strong, or his legs and seat too weak to drive the horse up to the hand, or the horse being asked to collect without enough impulsion. Other causes may be bad preliminary training, inconsistent contact on the reins, problems with sharp or wolf teeth. After the teeth have been checked it is corrected by riding the horse forward to a positive contact and with a forward feeling in the reins.

During training, many horses will drop **behind the**

vertical. This is not a serious fault as long as the horse has lowered his head and is not trying to avoid the contact but is maintaining a light, elastic, consistent feel with the hand. The tendency does, however, become serious if it is allowed to persist for a long period.

If the horse is **overbent** the highest point of the neck is no longer the poll, and the front of the face is behind the vertical, but in this case the horse takes too much contact and brings his chin in towards his chest. Through bad training he may have learnt to pull, possibly due to too strong and unyielding hands. The horse must be encouraged to take the hand forwards and may need to be worked on a much lighter contact.

Submission

The rider gradually increases his control over the horse to make him mentally willing and physically capable of obedience. The aim is a horse 'on the aids', i.e. accepting the aids in a relaxed manner and submitting without resistance to the will of the rider. Submission does not mean a reluctant subservience but the establishment of harmony between horse and rider.

The horse should learn to accept the aids from the legs without tension, the seat of the rider without stiffening, and from the reins without resistance. For these aids to be effective and their coordination possible they must go 'through' the horse: i.e. the horse's hindquarters, back, neck and mouth are coordinated and connected by an elastic-like circuit so that the aids applied in any one of the areas will be felt in all the others. If this firm, elastic connection is blocked at any point by stiffness, tension, or resistance (i.e. is not submissive throughout the body), the aids will not go 'through' and cannot be harmoniously combined. Also the horse's movement will be short of his best and any collection will tend to be a slowing down rather than a shortening and heightening of the steps.

To develop submission

To achieve mental submission the rider has to establish a rapport with his horse, and be able to communicate with him. To do this he must:

- Understand his horse – analyse his character, become aware of his physical strengths and weaknesses.
- Give the horse the best opportunity to understand: i.e. be able to ask clearly, to apply the aids effectively. To achieve this end, Chapters 5 and 6 should be thoroughly studied.

To arrive at physical submission the horse must develop impulsion, rhythm (and balance), suppleness, straightness and acceptance of the bit, so that he will find it easy to work 'with' and not 'for' his rider.

Improvement of the gaits

The gaits should improve as the above objectives are developed. It is important for the rider to have a clear idea of what is correct (Chapter 7). He can then prevent faults occurring, correct any which have occurred, and aim to improve the natural gaits. At the trot and canter one of the aims must be to make the gaits more cadenced: i.e. to develop a pronounced rhythm, more lift and expression, with energy to give more bounce to the strides through greater flexion of the joints and engagement of the hindquarters.

WARMING UP AND COOLING DOWN

Warming up

Throughout training it is necessary to warm the horse up prior to any work session. This loosening of the muscles is vital if the horse is expected to be able to work in a supple, compliant way, in both body and mind. No athlete can have a successful training or competitive session if he has not loosened up effectively, so that the muscles are warm, flexible and ready for further demands made on them.

The way in which a horse is warmed up may ultimately be modified a little to suit each individual horse and rider. However, the basic criteria are that:

- The horse is loosened systematically so that his muscles are relaxed and warm and ready for further work.
- The horse is mentally calm and attuned to the rider so that more demanding work can begin.
- The horse is physically and mentally able to accept and respond in the best way, to the discipline of the rider.

Warming up will usually include some or all of the following guidelines:

- Walk the horse on loose or long reins in a quiet area for 5 or 10 minutes.
- Walk the horse quietly up the road or similar, with or without other horses.
- The horse may be walked on a horse walker for 5 to 10 minutes prior to work.
- Lungeing can be used as a means of loosening and warming up but this should be in a long outline without the demands of short side-reins.
- The horse may be walked on a contact and moved through some simple lateral movements (leg yield, shoulder fore, quarters in) to begin to supple him.
- Some rising trot may follow any of the above walk work. The trot should be forward on fairly easy (long) reins, encouraging the horse to work confidently forward to seek the contact through a swinging back and a supple, loose frame.
- The horse may be worked quite forward and 'down' at this stage – this must never be confused with pushing the horse out of balance and onto his forehand, where the shoulders become more restricted and loaded. In this forward trot, the pace should be swinging without being hurried and the horse should show a looseness and freedom in his early connection from leg to hand.
- The canter may be used in the same way and the rider may choose to take a slightly lighter seat in the early canter to encourage the horse to start 'letting go' through his muscles, particularly those in his back.
- The time taken to loosen and warm the horse up will vary from horse to horse.
- Some young horses may take a long time to learn to 'let go'. Some older horses take longer to loosen than they did when they were younger.
- The relaxation of the mind is as important as that of the body, but finding the key can sometimes be difficult.
- An inattentive, anxious horse must be approached in whatever way ultimately achieves relaxation. There are no right or wrong answers here as long as the interests of the horse are paramount.

Cooling down

The period immediately after a demanding work session is as important as the warming up. After (ideally) a satisfactory moment on which to finish the work, the horse should be progressively cooled down.

- Straight after the last piece of demanding work, the horse may be encouraged to take the reins forward and down in either trot or canter.
- This is similar to the working-in practice. The horse is encouraged to stretch forward and down, thus alleviating the demands that have been made on the muscles, particularly in the hindquarters and back.
- The horse should not lose balance and quicken, falling onto his forehand; he should just take the rein forward and down while maintaining a balanced, swinging, rhythmical pace with active engagement of the hind legs.

- The horse may then be walked for several minutes to allow him to completely relax and dry off (if sweating) before returning to the stable.
- It is very important that the muscles should not be allowed to get cold. Depending on the time of year and the weather, the horse should be walked off, perhaps in a quarter sheet or sweat sheet.
- On returning to the stable he should be washed or sponged down, and/or brushed off and rugged according to his needs.
- It is as important that the rider does not neglect his own state after a work session. For example, he should put on a coat or waistcoat immediately after a work session so that he does not get suddenly cold.

SUMMARY

The above objectives should be borne in mind throughout the basic training of the horse. They should be the end products of work divided into two stages:

(1) preparatory, and
(2) intermediate.

CHAPTER 11

PREPARATORY TRAINING OF THE RIDDEN HORSE

The preparatory stage of training (lasting four to twelve months, depending on the ability of the horse and trainer) aims to produce a horse which:

- Has fine, regular and unhurried gaits.
- Is calm, relaxed and obedient to the aids of the rider.
- Shows a good natural outline, balance and rhythm.
- Moves freely forward, without collection, but with active hindquarters.
- Accepts the bit willingly, without tension or resistance.
- Remains straight when moving on straight lines and bent when moving on curved lines.
- Executes transitions smoothly and remains still when halted.
- Is a pleasure to ride in the school and out of doors.

The work

This should include:

- Work on the flat.
- Gymnastic jumping exercises.
- Riding out, including hill work.

WORK ON THE FLAT

Pattern of work. It is best to start at the rising trot on the horse's easier rein and then to change to the more difficult rein. The first part of the work is aimed at loosening up and relaxing the horse by working him down. All the work should be on both reins, and approximately equal time should be spent on each rein. Frequent rest periods at the walk on a long rein are needed, and it is wise to finish on a good note performing a movement that the horse can do well.

When the horse trots with lively steps and a relaxed swinging back he should begin to present a degree of roundness in his outline, with the poll at the highest point of his neck. When he has reached this stage he is ready for the sitting trot.

Duration. Half an hour to fifty minutes, or two sessions of thirty minutes are average sessions, but it depends greatly on the strength and temperament of the individual horse.

The figures

From this early stage of training it is important to get into the discipline of executing accurate figures.

The circles should be round, the straight lines straight, and the horse taken as deep into the corners as is possible without losing impulsion, rhythm, correct bend and the willingness to go forward.

The circles should be limited to 20m in diameter, the half circles to 15m in diameter, and the loops of a serpentine to 12m in diameter.

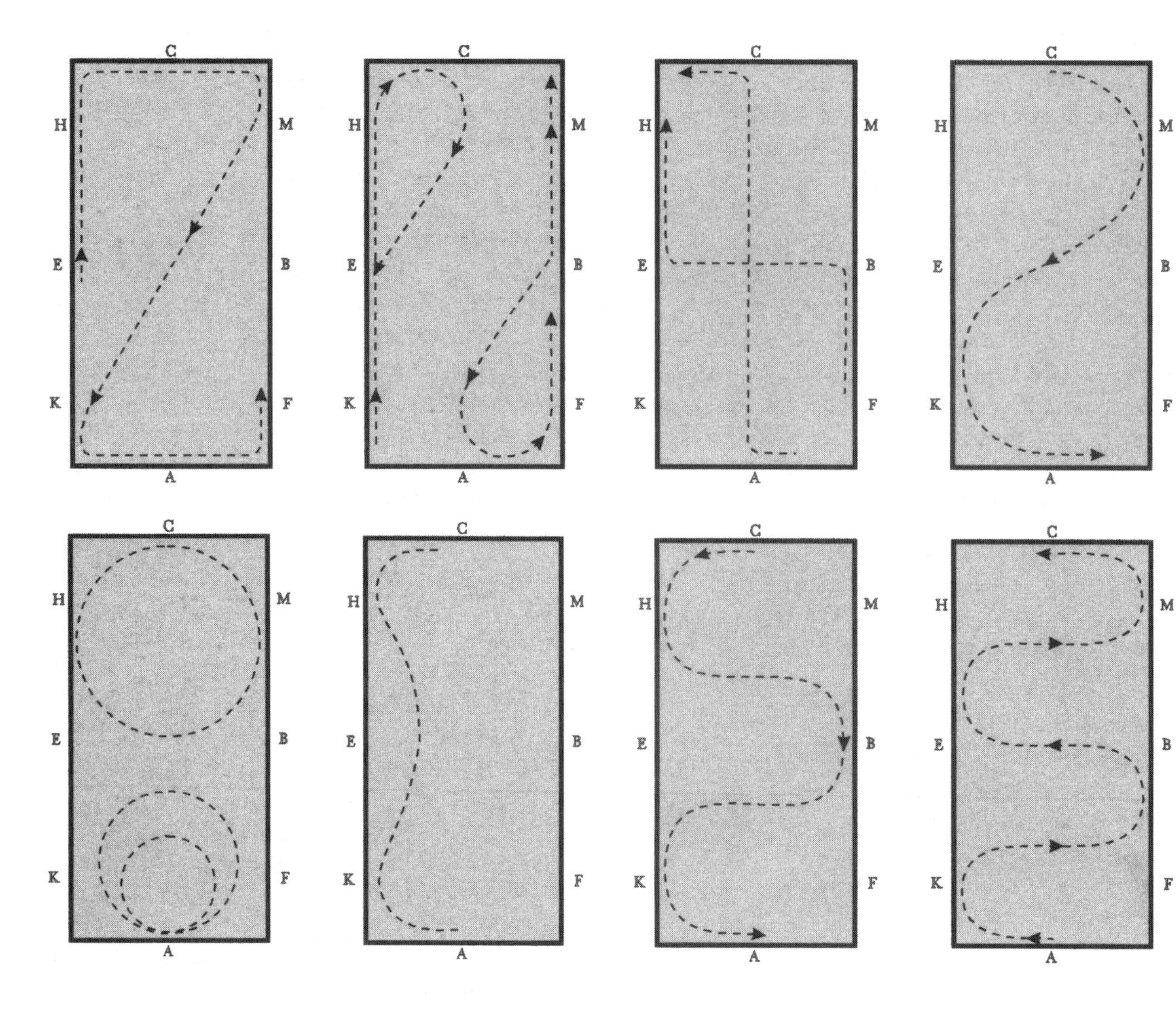

Figures used during work on the flat. Top row: methods of changing the rein. Bottom row, from left to right: 20m, 15m and 10m circles; shallow loop (5m); three-loop serpentine; four-loop serpentine.

The gaits

These should be limited to a free walk on a long rein, the medium walk, a working trot and working canter. (See Chapter 7.) When the horse is ready to canter he must learn to strike off on the correct leg. The easiest position for this is either when on a circle, or when going into the short side of the school. If he strikes off on the wrong leg he should not be made to halt – which he might regard as a form of punishment – but just to trot, and the strike-off should be tried again. If for any reason the horse when asked to canter goes into a fast trot, he should not be allowed to strike off until a calm, relaxed working trot has been established. Cantering is difficult for a young horse, especially on the circle, and should not be continued for too long. Many young horses find it easier to canter with their backs rounded and relaxed if the trainer is in a jumping position with his seat bones just out of the saddle.

The transitions

These should be progressive: i.e. not directly from canter to walk, but through trot, similarly with upward transitions. In the early stages of training, the manner in which a transition is executed is more important than its achievement at a given marker.

Transitions should be carried out smoothly but not abruptly. If the horse does not respond, ask again and again if necessary, so that the aids are repetitive, not continuous. For a transition to be satisfactory, the horse must be balanced as he goes into it, and must have sufficient impulsion. The rhythm of the gait should be maintained up to the moment that the gait is changed, or the horse is halted, and should be established in the new gait as soon as possible.

- Upward transitions (page 57). It is vital for the rider to prepare the young horse for an upward transition and, in particular, to develop enough impulsion to enable the horse to obey without throwing his head in the air or hollowing his back.
- Downward transitions (page 58). These must be ridden forward, the trainer maintaining his correct seat and using a restraining but allowing hand. If he pulls backwards on the reins he will create resistances and stiffen the horse's back. In the early stages it is helpful to use the voice to avoid having to pull on the reins.

Movements

These should be limited to the halt, the turn on the forehand, and an understanding of the half-halt.

The half-halt (see also page 58)

This is a hardly visible moderated version of the halt, which:

(a) Increases the attention and balance of the horse.

(b) Helps to engage the hindquarters, to generate impulsion, and to lighten the forehand.

(c) Warns the horse that the rider is about to ask something of him. To be effective, the rider must, as in all the work, get the horse to think forward: i.e. **the driving aids are more important than the restraining aids.** The seat and leg aids are applied to produce more activity in the hindquarters, which should have repercussions on other muscles in the horse's body (i.e. the muscles are coordinated, so the aids go 'through' and are not isolated to the hindquarters). To stop the driving aids simply increasing the horse's speed, the rein or reins momentarily restrain. This results in the increased energy and attention produced by the driving aids being contained within the horse, to result in (a), (b), and (c) above.

If the half-halt is to be effective, the horse's back must be **relaxed** and **swinging** to enable the aids to go 'through' and allow the back to perform its function of acting as a connecting link between the forehand and the hindquarters. If the back is **tense**, the rein aids cannot go 'through' and the tendency will be for the horse to raise his head, hollow his back and lose the engaging effect of the half-halt.

After applying the rein aid the rider then gives momentarily with the hands so that the horse learns to hold himself together and does not rely for support on the reins. At the intermediate stage the rider should aim to hold his horse with his seat and leg aids without reliance on the reins.

The half-halt becomes more important as training progresses, but the young horse should be gradually introduced to the aids and should learn to accept them correctly.

The halt (see also pages 57–58)

It is important from the beginning of the ridden work, for the novice horse to be taught to stand still when halted. Initially he should be halted largely through use of the voice and with a light contact on the bit; for a second or two he should not move his legs or head. The novice horse should not be asked to stand still for too long; about three seconds is enough. Too much importance should not be attached to the novice horse standing square. One hind leg is often left behind a little and it is better for the rider himself to remain still, rather than trying to correct the fault, which usually disappears as the horse becomes more supple and engaged. Not until the horse readily accepts the bit and is really going forward will he be able to bring his hind legs sufficiently under him to establish his balance and to stand with his weight equally adjusted over all four legs.

Gymnastic jumping exercises

These are discussed in detail in Chapter 14.

As soon as the horse has learned to accept the bit, and to walk, trot, and canter without excitement, he should receive elementary jumping lessons. They are valuable in teaching the horse to use himself athletically, thereby strengthening his muscles and making him both supple and mentally alert. They can be given about twice a week, on good going.

At this novice stage the jumps should be used to give a horse confidence and should never be too large. Work up from little fences to about 1m (3ft 3in.) in height, with a maximum of 1.5m (5ft) spread. Grids with accurately measured distances between the obstacles are initially the most valuable.

Riding out

It is vital to keep a young horse's interest. He will soon tire of school work if he is weak and finds it an effort. Riding out, especially hill work, will help to develop his muscles as well as providing him with the variety which will be mentally refreshing. Frequent riding out is, therefore, advisable, but the objects of training can still be kept in mind. Hacking across fields, over undulating ground, along lanes, need not be time off but another opportunity to develop the objectives of basic training.

In this outside work, control is vital. If it is lost the horse and rider will be frightened, so a trainer must gauge how much can be asked of his pupil. He should not ask a nervous horse to meet heavy traffic or other new, frightening experiences (e.g. farm machinery) without the company of another more reliable horse. If going for a canter he should sense when the horse is showing signs of 'coming to the boil', and ease the pace before he loses control; then the occasional gallop can be enjoyed with safety.

Visits to horse shows, where a young horse can get used to crowds, other horses and strange sights, are a useful experience. Towards the end of this stage of training, a day or two out with the local hunt can be beneficial, especially for potential eventers or jumpers who need to get accustomed to different obstacles, and for lazy horses to develop impulsion.

After riding out, the trainer should examine his horse in the stable for possible injury and in order to assess his general condition.

CHAPTER 12

INTERMEDIATE TRAINING OF THE RIDDEN HORSE

The intermediate stage is a continuation of the preparatory stage, further developing the objectives of training but with increasing emphasis being placed on collection.

Collection

Collection becomes an important objective at this stage, but it is only possible to develop if the trainer maintains and improves the other objectives:

- impulsion
- rhythm
- suppleness
- straightness
- acceptance of the bit
- submission, and
- good gaits

Benefits of collection

- The development and improvement of the horse's balance.
- The engagement and lowering of his hindquarters, which will lighten and make his forehand more mobile. This enables the strides to become longer or higher, as desired.
- The horse will develop more ease and self-carriage in his work which will make him more pleasant to ride.

The horse should become more manoeuvrable, more able to generate the power to extend his gaits, carry out dressage movements, and jump fences.

To collect

Collection is achieved by greater engagement of the hindquarters, and not a slowing down to produce trudging, inactive steps. When asking the horse to shorten and heighten his strides into collection, impulsion must be maintained, or even increased.

The major aids for collection are half-halts, increasingly small circles, serpentines, variations within

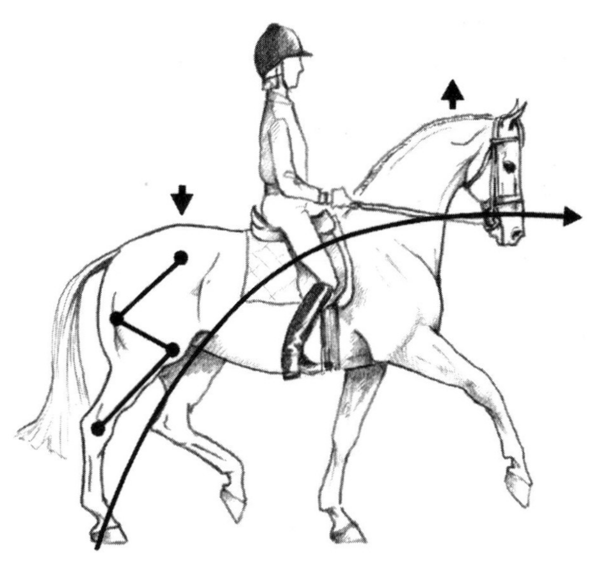

Developing impusion and carrying capacity (the ability to take weight onto the hindquarters).

a gait, smooth, direct downward and upward transitions, and lateral movements.

Work

This should include:

- Work on the flat.
- Gymnastic jumping exercises.
- Riding out, including hill work and some strong canters on good going.
- Competitions. If possible, occasional participation in such competitions as a one-day event of the type organised by the Riding Clubs, or Novice and Elementary dressage tests, or Novice show jumping. These would enable independent assessments of progress to be made.

WORK ON THE FLAT

The work first entails lengthening and loosening up the muscles, then flexing them into collection. When asking the horse for an effort, the trainer must first be certain of his aims and also that the horse is physically and mentally ready for the cooperation needed. If problems arise, revert to the basic principle of 'straighten your horse and ride him forward', as so many difficulties arise from loss of impulsion and crookedness.

The work must continue to be progressive, using the figures and movements shown below to improve the objectives of training. Thus from merely learning to remain immobile the horse can be taught to halt square and rein back; from the easiest lateral work of the turn on the forehand and leg yielding progress to the shoulder-in and half-pass; and from canter work in counter-canter and use of simple changes progress to flying changes.

Not only should the movements tackled be progressive but also the manner in which they are performed. Thus the trainer will progress from achieving just a few steps of a movement to quite lengthy phases of the movement; from performing, for example, shoulder-in with little collection finishing on a circle, to shoulder-in down the length of the school in greater collection, finishing with the horse being straightened back on the track; from riding half-pass with very little bend and very much forward, to asking for a good deal of bend and sideways movement. Although trainers should keep in mind how Grand Prix horses perform movements, they must realise that it takes considerable muscular power and suppleness to perform them this way. They can only be developed with progressive work. Also, few eventers or show jumpers would be able, or need, to develop the collection required for accurate Grand Prix dressage movements.

The figures

The trainer can gradually reduce the sizes of the circles as more collection is achieved to 10m diameter, and half circles of 6m diameter. The circles for the medium trot and medium canter should not be smaller than 20m diameter, and the extended canter should be ridden along straight tracks.

Serpentines are an excellent suppling exercise; the size of the loops can be gradually reduced. The serpentine can be used in trot, and in canter with simple changes on the centre line, or some counter-canter loops. For other useful movements see page 94.

Transitions

As long as they are performed correctly, frequent transitions from one gait to another, and transitions within the gait, help to achieve the objectives of training.

When working, the trainer can gradually increase the degree of collection in his horse and can alternate this successively with the medium and extended gaits. Transitions of two levels up – e.g. halt to trot, walk to canter – can be executed together with similar downward transitions.

The transitions should be made more quickly and less

progressively than in the preliminary stage.

Aims

- To show a clear transition.
- To be quick, but smooth and not abrupt.
- To maintain the rhythm of the gait up to the moment that the gait is changed, or the horse halts.
- For the new gait to be true and to show lively impulsion.
- For the horse to remain 'on the bit', light in hand, and calm.
- To remain balanced and 'on the bit'.

The halt (see also page 57)

Aims

At the halt in the preliminary stage the horse was first and foremost immobile, but not necessarily four square. Now the aims should be:

A good, square halt, with the horse remaining 'on the bit'.

- To distribute the weight evenly on all four legs which are pairs abreast of each other (a square halt).
- To hold the neck so that the poll is the highest point and the head is slightly in front of the vertical.
- To remain 'on the bit' and maintain a supple jaw.
- To remain motionless, but attentive, and ready to move off at the wish of the rider.

Execution

More of the horse's weight has to be transferred to his hindquarters by increasing the action of the rider's seat and legs, which should drive the horse towards a more and more restraining but allowing hand. By this intermediate stage the halt should be almost instantaneous, but not abrupt.

The rein-back

The horse moves backwards, raising and setting down his legs in almost diagonal pairs.

Aims

- To lift the feet off the ground so that the limbs are not dragged.
- To remain straight.
- To step back in a deliberate rhythm.
- To make all the steps the same length.
- To move forward without halting when asked.

Execution

The rein-back should not be asked for before the horse has become reasonably supple, flexible in his joints, and off his forehand, otherwise he will find it difficult and will have to be pulled back, which usually leads to a hollowing of the back and further resistances. If the horse does not respond in spite of being ready to learn to rein back, the rider must not pull him back, but

The rein-back.

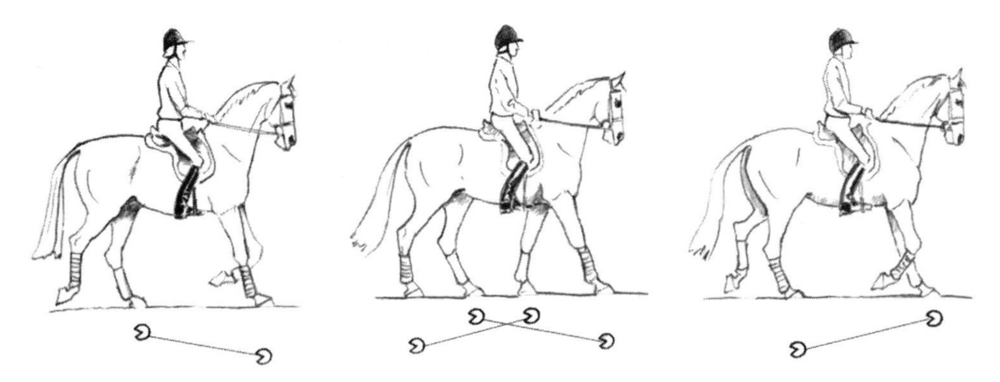

should push him on to a stronger contact.

The stages

- Practise frequent smooth transitions to the halt, with the horse standing four square and remaining on the bit.
- After a further good halt, apply the aids to move forward but with the hands restraining the forward movement. As the horse steps back, lighten the contact as a reward, but still keep him on the bit.
- One or two steps are sufficient in the early stages.
- After stepping back, the horse should walk forward without hesitation when asked to do so.
- The rider must control each backward step and vary the number for which he asks.

The rider

- Establishes a square halt and takes care that the horse remains on the bit.
- Eases the weight in the saddle by putting more weight into the stirrups and on the thighs.
- Applies the legs just behind the girth.
- Prevents the consequent inclination to move forward by restraining aids on the reins.
- Releases the pressure on the reins as soon as the horse steps back. It is vital that the rider does not pull backwards on the reins as the horse will then resist or run back stiffly. The horse must also be kept straight by appropriate use of the rider's legs and, if necessary, the reins.

The counter-canter

The rider asks the horse to travel in the opposite direction to that of the leading leg and bend, so that when on a curve to the left the horse canters with the right lead and vice versa.

Aims

- To maintain the bend to the leading leg so that the horse looks to the outside of the curve.
- To keep the hindquarters from swinging to the outside of the curve.
- To maintain the rhythm and balance.

Execution

The rider should only ask according to the suppleness and collection of his horse and should always bear in mind that the conformation of the horse does not allow him to be bent to the line of the circle. The early lessons can consist of loops off a straight line. Then progress, as the aims set about above are maintained, to circles and serpentines.

Benefits

- An important suppling and balancing exercise and improves straightness.
- Encourages the engagement of the hindquarters if carried out correctly.
- Can be of use when teaching flying changes.

The rider

- Uses the same aids as for the canter, maintaining the position towards the leading leg so that he will, for example, maintain position left when in counter-canter around a right turn. At first it may be necessary to hold this position more strongly, with the legs definitely applied and the weight positively to the inside, which is on the side of the leading leg.

Change of leg

To change the leading leg in the canter, the horse can do so through walk (simple change) and/or trot, or via a flying change.

Simple change

The horse carries out a transition directly to the **walk** and restarts into the canter with the other leg leading.

Simple change from left canter to right canter

Aims

- To execute the movement smoothly.
- To remain on the bit.
- To maintain impulsion.
- To keep the hindquarters engaged.
- To remain straight.

The rider

- Checks his position.
- Ensures that the canter is collected enough.
- Gives the aids to walk.
- After the walk has been established, changes his aids from position left to position right and gives the aid to canter right.

The flying change of leg

This takes place during a period of suspension in the canter when both fore and hind legs should change together, the leading hind leg initiating the change.

Aims

- To remain light, calm and straight.
- To maintain impulsion.
- To maintain the same rhythm and balance.
- To achieve a noticeable and clean jump from one leading leg to the other (i.e. the change has expression).

The flying change should not be attempted before:

- The horse's hindquarters are strong.
- The horse has the ability to collect at the canter and to maintain impulsion.
- The horse is balanced and straight.
- The horse remains 'on the bit' during his work.
- The canter strike-offs are correct.

Preparation

The horse should be asked to do simple changes at short

Flying change of leg in canter. (1) The left canter starts with the thrust of the right hind, then the left foreleg leads (2). During the moment of suspension (4), the change takes place and the new lead begins, with the thrust of the left hind (5).

intervals on alternate legs. When these are well performed with a degree of collection, the horse remaining straight and 'on the aids', the trainer should ask for alternately true and counter-canter through the walk.

Execution

To make the first flying change as easy as possible for the horse, he is usually cantered across the school on a diagonal in a well-balanced, well-collected canter, and asked to change at the end of the diagonal. If the change has been correctly made, the horse should first be settled before being rewarded with a walk on a long rein. If the change was not correct or not made at all, the rider might try once more and, if again it is a failure, he should return to the preparatory exercises before retrying. It is essential that the change should not be late behind: i.e. the change is made first with the forelegs and then a stride or more later with the hind legs. Unless the rider can feel such an error from the saddle, he should have an assistant on the ground to tell him whether the change has been correctly performed.

Timing: in the case of a simple change through another gait this is not difficult, but to perform a flying change this must take place during the moment of suspension which follows the use of the horse's leading foreleg. Only then are all four feet off the ground and only then can the horse answer the aids and change the leading hind leg and hence the sequence.

Flying change from left to right

The rider

- Checks his position.
- Makes a half-halt to improve the impulsion and balance and increase collection.
- Just before the leading leg comes to the ground he changes his aids from position left to position right without collapsing his hips.
- Makes sure he allows the horse's back muscles to swing.

It is important that the horse is kept straight and that the rider brings the new inside leg forward and the new outside leg back at the same moment. After the change the rider must keep the canter forward and active.

Alternative situations in which to ask for a change

Although many trainers teach their horses flying changes at the end of a diagonal, some horses find the following positions easier. If the horse does not change correctly at the end of the diagonal, then other options can be tried. Also, when continuing the training it is vital to ensure that a horse does not anticipate and start to change of his own accord. Therefore, ask for the change from different positions.

The alternatives

- From the counter-canter, which can be executed down the long side of the school. To prevent anticipation the rider should sometimes continue in the counter-canter beyond the points where he usually asks for a change. It is most important for the horse to remain straight throughout the movement and to avoid any sideways drift. It is important, too, for the horse to change on the aids and not to anticipate.
- From the canter half-pass allow one or two straight strides then ask for the change.
- In a serpentine ask for the change when crossing the centre line.
- From a 10m or 15m half circle ask for the change when just about to return to the track.

LATERAL WORK

Lateral work refers to any form of movement wherein at least one of the horse's hind feet follows in a different track from that of the fore feet. In lateral work the horse moves sideways as well as forwards. This helps to:

- Increase the obedience of the horse.
- Supple the horse, increasing the freedom of the shoulders, mobility of the hindquarters and the elasticity of that vital bond connecting the hindquarters, back, neck, poll and the mouth.
- To improve the cadence and balance.
- To help engage the hindquarters and so increase collection.

Aims

- Gaits to remain free and regular.
- To maintain impulsion, rhythm and balance.
- To achieve a slight bend from the poll to the tail

Turn on the forehand through 180 degrees.

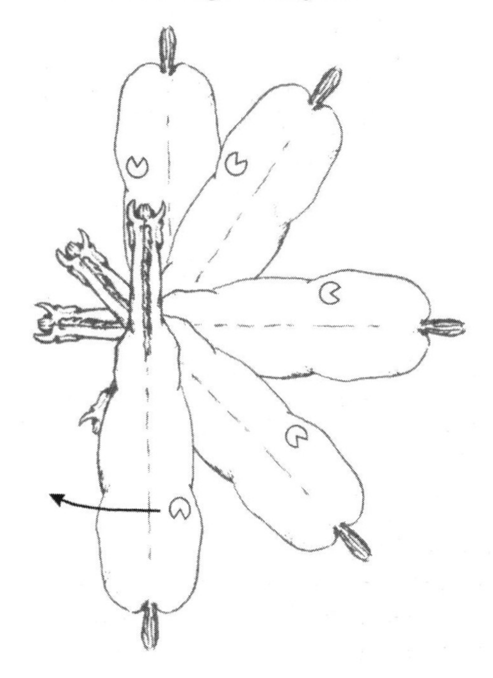

If the movement is carried out on the spot there is no engagement of the inside hind leg...

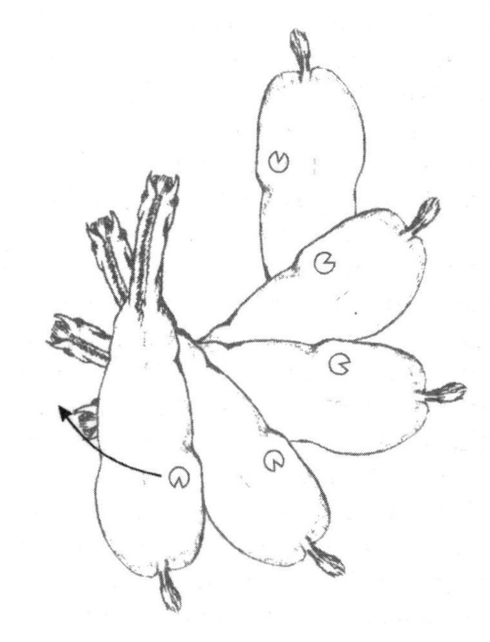

... it is better to walk around a small circle, since this will allow the inside hind leg to engage forward a little.

(except in leg yielding, when there is slight flexion only at the poll). The amount of bend depends on the suppleness and stage of training of the horse. It must never be so excessive (i.e. rider preoccupied with going sideways) that fluency, balance and impulsion are inhibited.

The turn on the forehand (see page 103)

The horse's hindquarters rotate around the forehand, away from the direction of the bend (see illustrations on previous page). This exercise is used to teach the rider the use of different leg and rein aids and teaches the horse to move away from the leg.

The rider

- Corrects his position.
- Maintains the walk or halts momentarily.
- Indicates the direction by asking for a slight bend to the inside and brings his weight slightly on to the inside seat bone.
- Applies vibrant pressures with his inside leg on the girth, or, with a novice horse, very slightly back to encourage him to step sideways. Brings the outside leg slightly further behind the girth, where it can be applied to control the movement if the horse starts to move around too fast.
- Uses the outside rein to restrain the forward movement and to prevent the horse bending too much in the neck.
- Turns the body slightly in the direction of the bend. On completing the movement the horse is ridden forward by closing the outside leg and allowing with the hands.

Throughout the turn coordination of the seat, legs and hands will make sure that the horse stays between the hand and leg and makes a supple turn, not evading forwards or backwards.

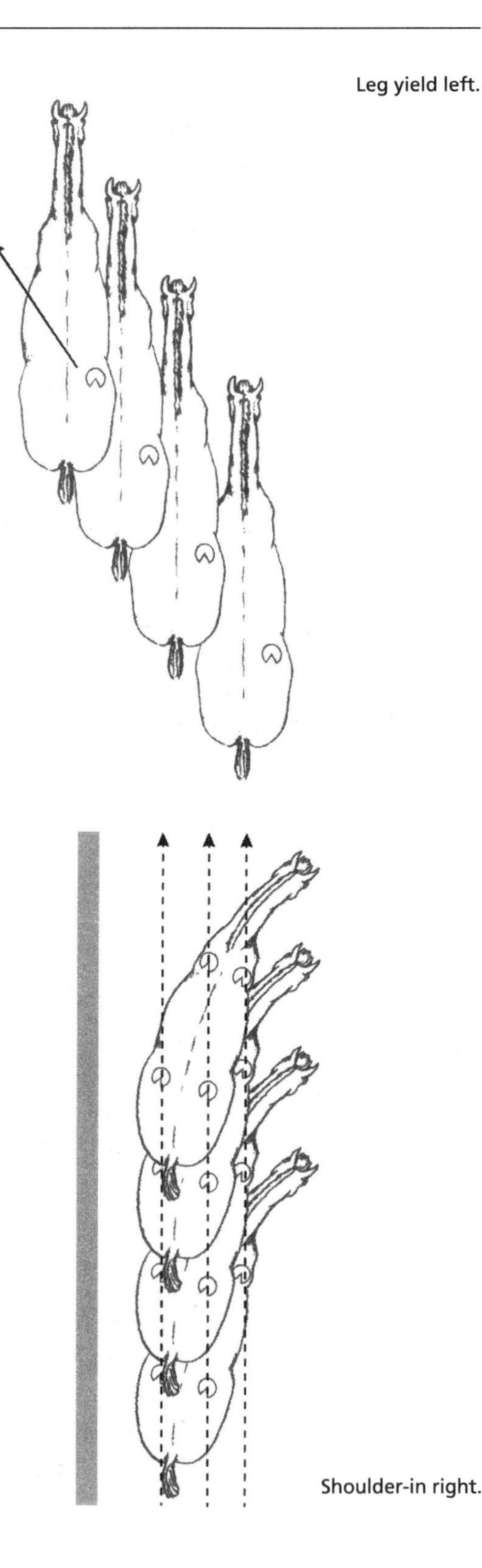

Leg yield left.

Shoulder-in right.

An alternative: The turn on the forehand ridden in the above manner results in the horse moving his hindquarters away from the direction of the bend. The turn on the forehand can also be executed by reversing the aids, when the rider's outside leg becomes the dominant one to cause the horse to step forward and in front of the inside hind leg as in travers (see page 107); the horse then moves the hindquarters in the direction of the bend.

Leg yielding (see page 104)

In the leg yield the horse moves forward and sideways. He should be straight, except for a slight flexion at the poll, allowing the rider to see the eyebrow and nostril on the inside. This bend is in the opposite direction to that in which he is moving. The inside legs pass and cross the outside legs. It is the easiest of the lateral movements, requiring no collection, and is therefore especially valuable in the training of young horses. It is used by many trainers as a means of introducing lateral work. It is a movement which has caused controversy, and not all trainers are in agreement about its use.

Execution

The first lessons are best given at the walk. Only when the horse understands the aids should it be tried at the trot. The usual figures for trying the leg yield are:

- From a 10m circle leg yield out to either the long side of the arena or to start a 20m circle.
- From the short side of the arena turn down the centre line and leg yield to the long side.
- Along the diagonal when the horse should be as close as possible parallel to the long side but with the forehand just in advance.
- Along the wall when the horse should not be at a greater angle than 35° to the direction in which he is moving.

As the most basic of the lateral movements, leg yielding can be carried out in walk and working trot. Hence, many riders and/or horses start lateral work with this exercise.

The rider

- Corrects his position.
- Applies the inside leg by the girth. This is the dominant leg, causing the horse not only to step forward but also to bring his inside hind leg further under his body and slightly in front of the other hind leg.
- Keeps his outside leg just behind the girth and applies when necessary to keep the horse straight and to maintain the forward movement.
- Asks with the inside rein for a slight flexion at the poll so that he can see the eye and arch of the nostril.
- Uses the outside rein to regulate the flexion to help balance the horse and prevent the shoulder from falling out.

Shoulder-in (see page 104)

In shoulder-in the horse moves at an angle of about 30° to the direction of the movement, with his whole body bent slightly, around the rider's inside leg, while looking away from the direction in which he is moving. The horse's inside foreleg passes and crosses in front of the outside leg; the inside hind leg is placed in front of the outside leg. It can be executed on straight lines or circles. It is most commonly performed in trot, and can be ridden in walk and canter to help straighten the horse.

Benefits

The shoulder-in is the foundation of all collected and advanced lateral work. Because of this, it is perhaps the most valuable of all exercises available to the trainer:

- It is suppling and collecting movement, as the inside hind leg is brought well under the body and placed in front of the outside. To do this the horse must lower his inside hip and flex the joints of the hind leg.

- It helps the rider to control the shoulder of the horse. By 'thinking shoulder-in' when riding turns and circles, and particularly before striking off to canter, it helps to prevent the shoulder falling out or the quarters coming in.
- It helps to make the horse straight.
- It improves the quality of the gaits.
- It can be used to discipline a horse.

Aims

- To maintain impulsion and willingness to go forward.
- To maintain rhythm.
- The bend should be through the body and not just the neck, otherwise the collecting value is lost and the shoulders tend to fall out.
- The hindquarters should not swing out (that is quarters-out instead of shoulder-in).
- The movement itself should go 'through' the horse: that is, the elastic bond between the hindquarters and mouth is maintained at all times.

Common faults in shoulder-in.

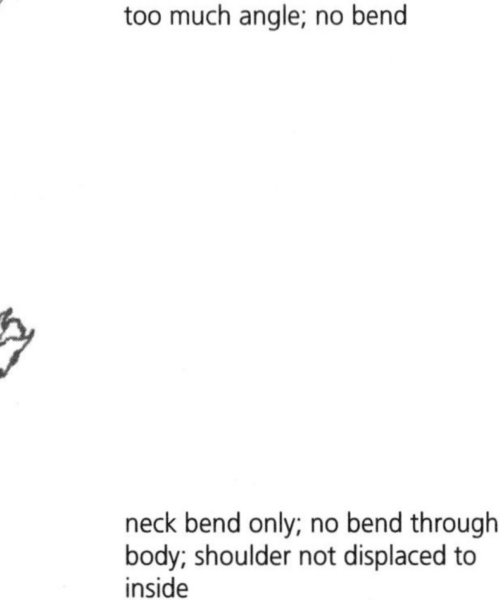

Execution

Sometimes a first lesson is given at the walk, but as soon as the horse understands what is wanted, the movement should be executed at the trot. The usual way to begin the movement is on completion of a corner before the long side of the school. Instead of riding down the long side the rider continues on the curve of the corner, bringing the forehand away from the track but keeping the hind legs still on the track, where they should remain throughout the movement. The rider when guiding the forehand off the track increases the pressure from his inside leg and the restraining action of the outside rein, while maintaining the bend with the inside rein and controlling the hindquarters with the outside leg.

At first, only a few steps of shoulder-in should be asked for, followed by the horse being ridden forward on a single track in the direction he was facing. The number of steps can be increased as performance and suppleness improve.

In shoulder-in the horse moves forwards and sideways on three tracks. He is bent around the rider's inside leg and moves away from the direction of the bend (see illustration on page 104). The horse must be able to show some engagement of the hind legs so that the gait is developing some collection.

The rider

- Checks his position.
- Improves the impulsion and balance with a half-halt.
- Indicates the bend and direction with the inside rein.
- Increases the pressure of the inside leg on the girth to maintain the bend and further engage the horse's inside hind leg.
- Contains this extra impulsion by closing the fingers on the opposite (outside) rein, so preventing the horse from stepping straight forward and regulating the bend, particularly to prevent excessive neck bend.
- Rests his outside leg a little further behind the girth than his inside leg to support the bend and stop the hindquarters swinging out, just as on a circle.
- Turns his body slightly to the inside.
- Transfers slightly more weight to the inside.
- Keeps upright and in balance with the horse.

When the shoulder-in is correctly ridden, it should be possible to abandon the inside rein for a few steps without the horse losing his balance, impulsion, or rhythm.

If and when the rider's outside hand allows the horse to move straight forward again, he should do so immediately and return to a circle. However, in a dressage test the horse is usually brought back straight on the track or ridden into a movement such as medium trot.

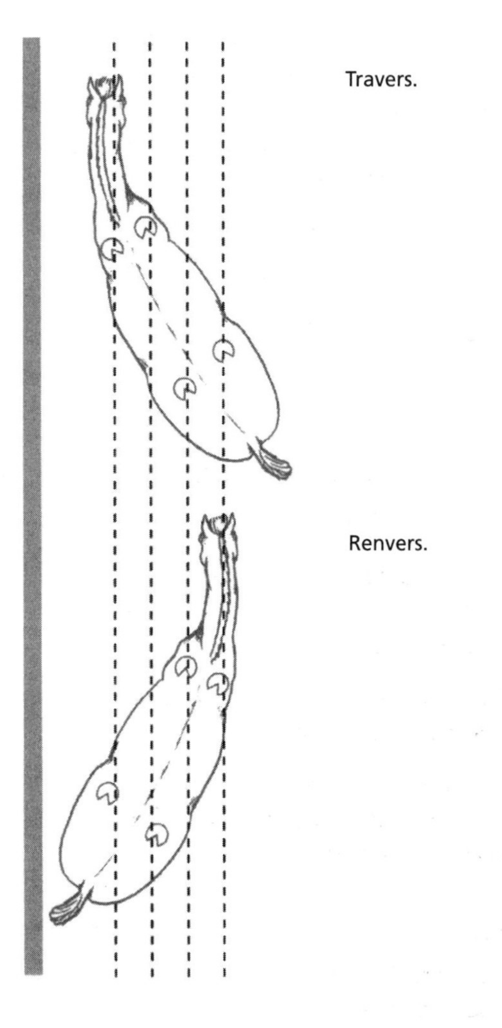

Travers.

Renvers.

The travers and renvers

In the travers (quarters-in) and the renvers (quarters-out) (shown above), the horse is slightly bent around the inside leg of the rider and positioned at an angle of about 30° to the line of the track. They differ from the shoulder-in in that the horse looks in the direction in which he is moving. They can be performed along the wall or centre line. Primarily ridden in walk and trot, but can be used in canter too.

Benefits

- To increase obedience.

- To prepare for the half-pass.
- To increase the control over the hindquarters.
- As a collecting exercise in the canter they can be used in the preparation for the pirouette.

Execution

The early lessons are usually given in the walk, but can later be carried out at trot and canter.

To execute travers: at the end of the short side, instead of straightening on to the track, the bend of the turn is maintained and the aids for travers are applied.

As the renvers is an inverted travers it uses the same muscles etc. as the travers.

The aids for travers and renvers are identical apart from the original positioning of the horse.

The rider

- Checks his position.
- Improves the balance and impulsion with a half-halt.
- Asks for a bend with the inside rein and leg.
- Applies his outside leg behind the girth to move the hindquarters over.
- Controls the impulsion and the amount of bend with the outside rein.

The half-pass

This is a variation of travers, executed on the diagonal (see diagram above right). The horse is slightly bent around the inside leg of the rider and should be aligned as nearly as possible parallel to the long side of the school, but with the forehand slightly in advance of the hindquarters. At trot and walk the outside legs cross and pass in front of the inside legs, but at the canter it is usual for the legs not to cross. The horse looks forward and sideways in the direction in which he is moving. The half-pass can be ridden at all three gaits.

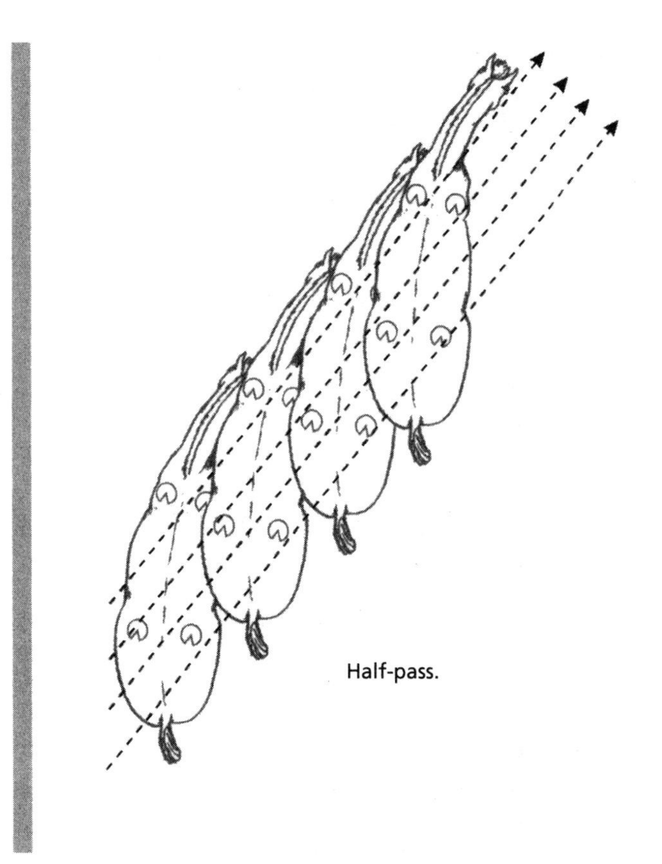

Half-pass.

Aims

- To maintain the same balance and rhythm throughout the entire movement.
- To maintain a bend, but this must not be so excessive that it leads to a loss of impulsion.
- To ensure the forehand is light so that there is freedom and mobility in the shoulders and ease and grace to the movement.

Execution

Correct execution depends greatly on how the horse goes into the movement and how well the forward element predominates. The trainer might begin the lesson with a half-volte followed by the half-pass. A useful alternative is shoulder-in along the short side and, as the corner is turned, half-pass across the diagonal; or to leg yield from the centre line to the long side and return to the centre line in half-pass.

The aids are similar to those for travers and renvers.

The rider

- Checks his position.
- Improves the horse's balance and impulsion with a half-halt.
- Puts the horse into position right, or left, taking the forehand fractionally off the track.
- Looks and turns his body towards the point to which the movement is being made.
- Puts more weight into the inside stirrup.
- Keeps the forward movement and bend with the inside leg.
- Maintains the bend with the inside rein.
- Applies the outside leg behind the girth to encourage both the horse's outside legs to step forward and across the front of the two inside legs with rhythmical variations of pressure.
- Uses the outside rein to control the amount of forward movement and to prevent too much bend.

As the movement progresses, the outside leg aids are gradually increased so that the horse is finally straight (i.e. parallel) to the track or wall before being ridden forward on one track, or before changing to a half-pass on the other rein.

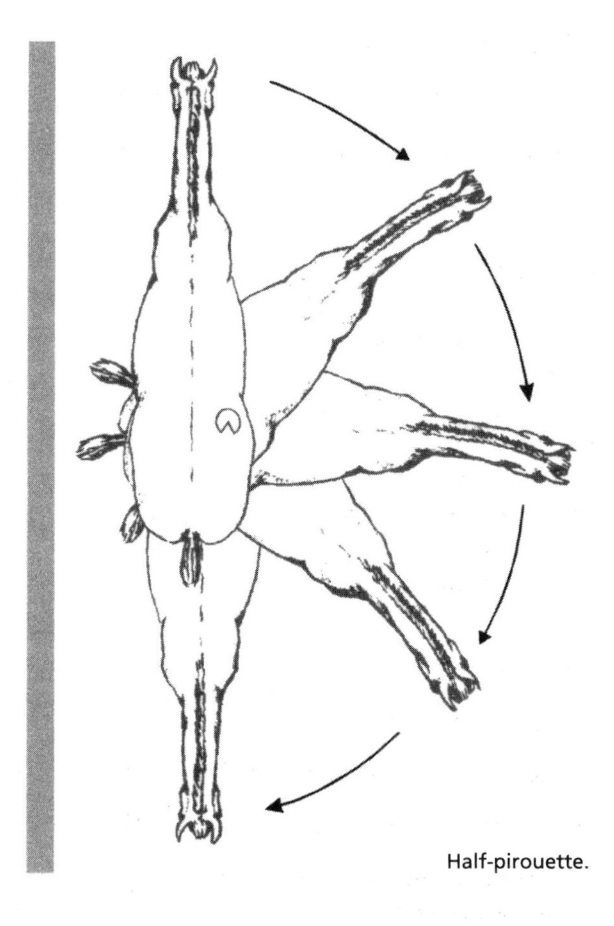

Half-pirouette.

Half-pirouette at the walk

This is a half circle performed on two tracks with a radius equal to the length of the horse. The forehand moves around the haunches. The forefeet and the outside hind foot move around the inside hind foot, which acts as the pivot, returning to the same spot or just in front of it each time it is lifted.

Aims

- The horse should be slightly bent to the direction in which he is moving.
- To remain on the bit.
- To maintain the rhythm of the walk.
- The horse should not move backwards.

Execution

The horse can be taught to respond to the aids for the walk pirouette by at first asking him for travers on a small circle. As he manages to retain the impulsion and sequence of the walk footfalls the size of the circle can be reduced until it becomes a walk pirouette.

INTRODUCING THE DOUBLE BRIDLE

The double bridle puts finishing touches, or the final polish, on movements which have already been taught and well executed when ridden in a snaffle. It can be worn after the horse has been introduced to lateral work and is accepting the bit in all work. Its first introduction should be with some simple work on a single track. Variations of pace within a gait will help to establish good impulsion and will encourage the trainer to ride the horse on to the bit. The frequency of the use of the double bridle depends upon the rider and the horse.

SUMMARY

When the horse is able to perform well all the school movements of the intermediate stage he should be a very good ride. It is a level of training which would benefit show jumpers; advanced event horses have to be able to do the work in order to perform the FEI Three-Day-Event Test.

More advanced training on the flat is not important for show jumpers or eventers, so the next chapter is usually treated as the sphere of the specialist dressage horse.

CHAPTER 13 ADVANCED TRAINING ON THE FLAT

At this stage the rider/horse partnership begins to specialise. If dressage is chosen, ultimately 'The dressage rider is an artist and the horse is his medium; together they produce a work of art' (Hans Handler). Only the great riders and horses can achieve this, but it should still be the aim of everybody embarking on this advanced training.

The more particular aims at this stage should be to train the horse to be:

- Responsive to delicate aids.
- Exceptionally supple in all gaits and movements.
- Able to generate great impulsion and collection.

To achieve these aims the rider must become:

- An analyst who pays great attention to detail and is quick to recognise faults and problems.
- Open-minded – ready to admit an error, eager to learn and, if necessary, willing to adjust his means of achieving the ends.
- Dedicated and able to work with enthusiasm day after day.
- Aware that no horse can perfect his movements unless he is skilfully ridden. The rider's balance, posture and correct application of aids become critical and can only be developed and maintained through great determination and discipline.

Facilities

At this stage, regular work is vital. It should be on good going, as hard, rough ground jars the horse and stiffens his back. It is also important to have enough space to develop the extensions. Therefore, either a large indoor school or outdoor arena 20m x 60m becomes a practical necessity.

Assistance

Help from a knowledgeable person on the ground is vital, not necessarily every day, but regularly, to check the rider's position and the horse's paces and movements.

Horsemastership

Attention to detail includes the care of the horse, who needs:

- To be well fed as he must be very fit to do advanced work.
- Consistent grooming to keep him clean and to tone up his muscles.
- Constant attention to his physical well-being as strains, sores, etc., if not put right, will affect his work.

Objectives of training

The objectives remain the same as previously stated (page 85), though some should be nearer to achieving success than others. Thus, by this stage the horse should be submissive, straight, accepting the bit and secure in his rhythm in all three gaits. The major areas for improvement will be:

- suppleness
- impulsion
- collection

General school work

With the possible exception of the turn on the forehand, all the exercises of the Intermediate stage can be included in this basic school work.

The gaits

More time can be spent on the walk to develop the variations within this basic gait. The collected and extended walk must be developed, but with great care. An assistant on the ground should check that the sequence of footfalls remains true, for the rhythm is all too easily lost with so little impulsion being produced at the walk.

Greater variations within the trot and canter should be asked for, but taking care to develop enough impulsion to make this possible without hurrying in the extensions, or slowing down in the collections.

Circles

Ridden at the collected trot and canter these can be gradually reduced in size from 10m diameter to 6m diameter (a volte).

Aims

- The hindquarters should not swing inwards or outwards.
- To avoid excessive bend in the neck.
- Horse and rider should not lean in (or out).
- Rhythm is maintained during and when entering and leaving the circles.
- To perform circles equally well on both reins.

Serpentines

These should by now be relatively easy suppling exercises at the collected or working trot, and useful variations can be used at the canter. Loops can be performed at the counter-canter as well as at the true canter, and the width of the loops can be reduced as the horse becomes more collected, so that the exercise becomes progressively more difficult: i.e. use a four-loop serpentine in a 20m x 60m arena at first and then progress to six loops. Flying changes can be executed on the centre line of the serpentine; however, simple changes are also a most useful suppling exercise and continually confirm submission and obedience.

Aims

- The loops to be of a similar size and shape.
- Simple or flying changes to be executed fluently and accurately.
- Rhythm to be maintained.
- Correct bend to be maintained.

Transitions

The following direct transitions can be practised:

Upward transitions

- Halt to collected trot.
- Rein-back to collected trot or canter.
- Collected walk to collected canter.
- Halt to collected canter.

Later:

- Piaffe to collected trot.
- Piaffe to passage.

Downward transitions

- Extension to collection at all three gaits.
- Collected walk, collected canter, and collected and medium trot to halt.

Later:

- Passage or piaffe to halt.

Aims
As on page 95.

Lateral work

The half-pass, travers and renvers should be executed with a greater degree of collection and sideways movement, but only insofar as the essential impulsion and fluency are maintained.

Counter change of hand (zigzag)

The counter change of hand (zigzag) is a series of half-passes either side of a line.

To execute at the trot
From a half-pass to the right the rider's outside (left) leg is used to direct the hindquarters slightly further over to the right and at the same time the horse's bend is changed so that the forehand can take the lead. The aids are then applied for a half-pass to the left. This will ensure that in the first steps of half-pass into the new bend on each occasion, the shoulders will very slightly be in advance of the quarters. Allowing the quarters to lead into a half-pass is a bad fault.

To execute at the canter
From a half-pass to the right the rider stops driving the horse laterally and rides him straight forward for two or three strides, during which time he asks for the change and the new bend to the left before applying the aids for the half-pass left. When the horse can perform the change fluently and equally well from right to left half-pass or vice versa, the number of straight strides can be reduced to ultimately one, when the new bend is asked for during the change.

Aims

- The forehand must always lead in the half-pass.
- The horse must take strides of equal length in both directions of the half-pass.
- Impulsion, rhythm and balance must be maintained throughout the movement.

Flying changes in series

When the horse can execute single flying changes on the aids and in balance he should be ready to start a series of flying changes, which are executed regularly after a given number of strides. The number of strides between changes can be reduced as he masters the easier series from, say, five to two (two-time changes) and finally to changes every stride (one-time changes).

Execution
In these series the degree of collection should be slightly less than in the collected canter to ensure a good forward bound at each change.

One particular series should not be practised for too long, as the horse then tends to anticipate and will not change on the aids. The series and the number of changes asked in any series should be varied.

If teaching a more difficult series, end the lesson on one that is easy for him: that is, perform some four-time changes after doing some two- or one-time ones.

Aims

- Keeping the horse straight. Any tendency to drift or swing should be corrected by:

  (a) Guiding the forehand, 'thinking shoulder-in', as each change is asked for.

  (b) Increasing the impulsion, riding forward into the changes at a stronger canter: using the inside leg to achieve this.

- The change to be executed with the forelegs and hind legs changing simultaneously. If the change is late behind, this is usually due to either the horse being on his forehand or to the rider using too much rein and not enough leg. More impulsion and collection should be generated.
- Rhythm and impulsion must be maintained. If the horse moves more and more slowly through the series he should be ridden forward and asked to change at a medium canter. If he moves more and more quickly, half-halts should be applied during the strides when he is not changing.

Canter pirouette

The pirouette (half-pirouette) is a circle (half circle) performed on two tracks, the circle having a radius equal to the length of the horse. The forehand moves around the hindquarters, the forefeet and the outside hind foot moving around the inside hind foot which is lifted and put down again on the same spot, or slightly in front of it.

Aims

- To keep the horse 'on the bit' with a light contact and a slight bend to the direction in which he is turning.
- To maintain balance, rhythm and impulsion.
- To maintain the regularity of the canter hoof beats. The inside hind leg is lifted and returned to the ground in the same rhythm as the outside hind foot, and should not remain on the ground.
- The strides should be accentuated, cadenced, and for a full pirouette should be six to eight in number and for a half-pirouette three to four.

The rider

- Collects the horse by a series of half-halts.
- Uses similar aids to those for half-pass, except the length of the stride is adjusted to reduce forward movement and produce a half-pass on the smallest circle.

Pirouettes and half-pirouettes may be ridden at the walk and later at the canter, but can only be achieved at the trot in piaffe.

Execution

The pirouette at the canter is one of the most difficult of all the advanced movements, as it calls for a high degree of collection and great impulsion. Horses should only be taught pirouettes after they have developed a good collected canter full of impulsion, are responding correctly to the half-halt, and are able to shorten the canter so much that for a few strides they almost remain on the spot (still in three-time) before willingly going forward again.

Various methods

- From a large walk pirouette and one in which the hindquarters are very well engaged, strike off into the canter while maintaining the same aids as for the walk pirouette. The horse should canter pirouette for a few steps before cantering straight forward (if he lacks impulsion) or returning to the walk (if he becomes excitable). The success of this method depends on the strike-off being of high quality.
- From the renvers. At the end of a long side the rider asks for a very small half circle (or passade) to canter in renvers parallel to the long side, and then turns towards the wall to perform a three-quarter pirouette. This method enables better control over the outside hind leg at the moment of starting the pirouette (one of the commonest faults is for the hindquarters to swing outwards). Also, the horse is already in the correct bend.
- From a large circle. This can be more difficult, as it is not so easy to prevent the hindquarters falling out, but is a useful progression after the above two methods towards a pirouette on a single track. Voltes are performed within the large circle, eventually

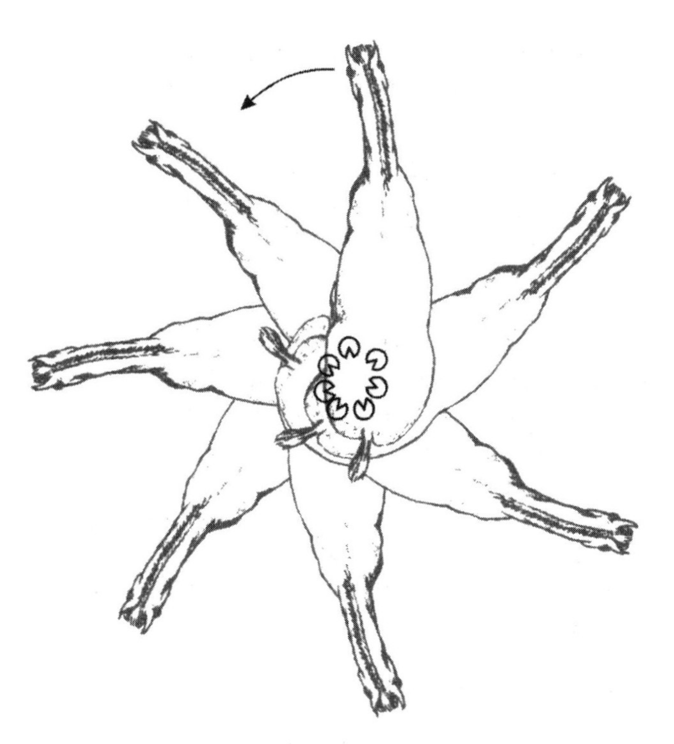

Pirouette: in theory the horse should lift and set down the inside hind on exactly the same spot, but in practice the inside hind leg makes a very small circle. The smaller this circle, the better the pirouette.

making them so small they become a passade and finally, a half-pirouette. Then proceed in counter-canter before trying on the other rein.

- From travers on a large circle, or from half-pass.
- From a straight line, but this should not be tried until the horse performs a satisfactory pirouette in the above methods. The rider should give his horse a slight shoulder-in position when approaching the point to which the pirouette is to be carried out, and the canter highly collected so that he is almost cantering on the spot when he is asked to turn into the pirouette.

If during attempts at the pirouette, the horse moves into the walk, it is important to keep asking with the aids for the pirouette, but with more vigour so that he returns to the canter. If he starts to swing around quickly, to swivel on his inside hind leg, return to work at the travers or renvers so that control over every collected stride can be maintained. Also, he can be asked to walk during the pirouette, perform a few steps of the pirouette at walk and then strike off into the canter, still in the pirouette when more control over each stride should have been established.

It is vital during the pirouette for the rider to retain the correct position, to remain upright with his seat in the saddle and to avoid tipping forward or to the outside with the momentum of the movement.

When working on pirouettes it is important to remember that they are demanding on the horse and should not be attempted for too long. It is important, too, for the size of the pirouette to be varied from half to three-quarter to whole, so that the horse remains on the aids and ready to come out of it whenever asked.

Piaffe

This is a highly collected, elevated and cadenced trot nearly on the spot.

Aims

- The height of the toe of the raised foreleg should be level with the middle of the cannon bone of the other foreleg, the forearm lifts towards the horizontal. The toe of the raised hind leg should reach just above the fetlock joint of the other hind leg.
- The neck should be raised and arched, the head perpendicular, the back supple and swinging, and the hindquarters slightly lowered, with active hocks well engaged to give great freedom, lightness and mobility to the shoulders and forehand.
- Each diagonal pair of legs should be raised and returned to the ground alternately with an even rhythm and a definite, but short, period of suspension.
- The piaffe should be produced as a result of great impulsion, so the horse should be ready and willing to move forward at all times.
- The horse should not move backwards, cross the

Piaffe. Maximum collection and enagement of the lowered hindquarters. There should be activity of the hind legs, lightness of the forehand, and proud submission.

forelegs, swing the forehand, or hindquarters, or take irregular steps.

- The horse should remain 'on the bit' with a supple poll and a light, but taut, rein.

The rider

- Corrects his position.
- Uses both legs by the girth, either together or alternately, to ride forward into a restraining hand, but still with an allowing, light rein contact. The object is to ask the horse to bring both hind legs a little further under his body and so to lower his hindquarters and round his back.
- Sits lightly to allow the horse to round and move 'through' his back, but in an erect position, with the seat bones forward to encourage forward impulsion.
- As the horse comes into piaffe, indicates the rhythm by increasing and decreasing the pressure of his legs without removing them from the horse's sides. Once the horse has understood, the rider must be careful to take up the rhythm offered by the horse.

A well-trained horse in correct equilibrium will only require a light but consistent contact with the rein to hold it in piaffe, and should always be ready to move straight forward into passage or another gait.

At an intermediate standard, the horse should be allowed to gain a little ground, but advanced horses should stay on one spot for ten to twelve steps.

Execution

The piaffe can be taught either from the ground or from the saddle. In the former method it is easier for the horse to use his back without the weight of the rider, but some horses find the latter easier to understand.

Teaching from the ground

These lessons should take place in an enclosed arena and the stages are as follows:

1. The horse is brought to the middle of the arena, fitted with a snaffle, saddle, cavesson, lunge rein and side-reins. The side-reins should be adjusted so that they just make contact when the horse is collected. It may be necessary to shorten them as he becomes more collected. The lunge rein is attached to the

cavesson and the horse is taken to the track on the left rein, as this is the easiest for most horses and convenient for the trainer.

2. The trainer positions himself near the shoulder of the horse. Taking up a fairly short rein in his left hand and holding the whip in his right hand he walks the horse slowly once or twice around the arena. As soon as the horse is walking in a calm and relaxed manner, he can be asked to trot. The hind legs should initiate this transition and the steps should be short. If the horse tries to go forward too much, the trainer should apply restraining aids with the hand. If the horse is reluctant to go forward, touch him with the whip just above the hind fetlocks. The voice should be used to supplement these driving and restraining aids. When the horse can work calmly and with rhythm in this exercise, the teaching of piaffe can begin.

3. With the horse standing correctly at halt on a long side of the arena, the trainer should position himself, as before, alongside the shoulder of his horse with his whip in his right hand. He will now take up a very short rein, holding his left hand closely behind the head of his horse (see below). From the halt the horse should be asked to move forward with a few steps of very collected trot and then brought again to the halt; this time the trainer should move to stand directly in front of his horse. The horse will soon come to understand that the trainer at his side means activity, and that the trainer in front means immobility.

   Eventually the aim must be for the horse to work on both reins, but for the first day the trainer may be satisfied with a few good steps on one rein. Over a series of lessons the trainer should progressively ask the horse to shorten the trot strides and should increase the collection. The hind legs must come further under the body; to encourage them to do so and to spring elastically off the ground, the trainer can use the whip to touch the hind legs. Only a few strides at a time should be asked for in this manner.

4. When seven or eight perfectly level steps can be

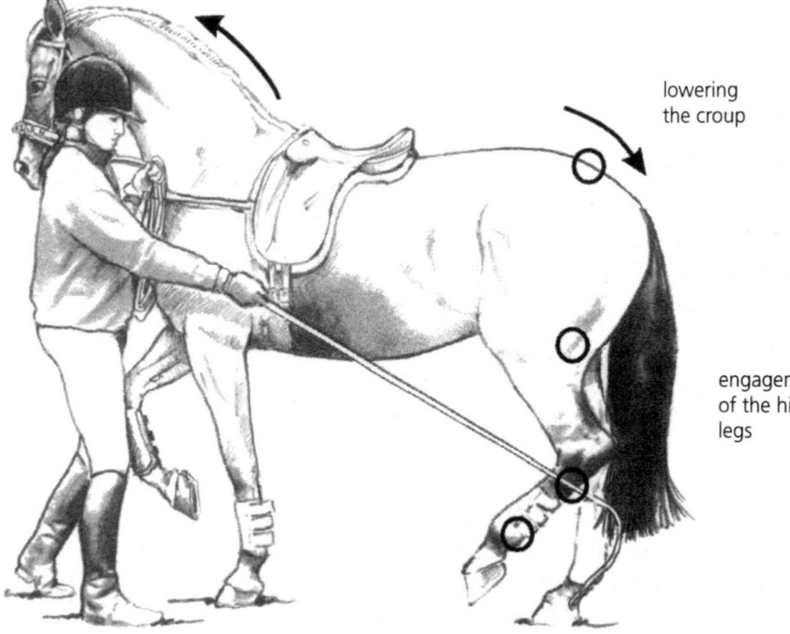

Training piaffe from the ground.

executed without moving forward further than one yard, the horse may be ridden: but the rein should still be in the hands of the trainer, who continues to control the horse from the ground in the same manner as before. Eventually, the trainer can ride the horse to perfect the movement.

The trainer's main considerations should be:

- Never to ask too much. The horse has to work hard to produce the necessary impulsion and bouncy spring to his action, so the lessons should not last too long and should end if possible, on a good, calm note.
- The horse must remain straight. If he tries to bring his hindquarters from the wall, the trainer should counter with a slight shoulder-in position.
- The strides must be level. The trainer should never sacrifice levelness through efforts to produce more elevated steps.
- The horse should always move forward – if only one inch per step – until training has reached its final stage, when 10 to 12 steps on the spot will be the aim.
- The hind legs should not be brought too far under the body or the hindquarters will be over-burdened. The horse will then have difficulty in lifting his hind feet off the ground which tends to make the trot irregular and the forward transitions abrupt.

Teaching from the saddle

This method, although usually easier for the trainer (since he should have more control), makes it more difficult for the horse to use his back elastically.

The principal considerations and progressive training methods are similar to those outlined in training from the ground. An assistant trainer walks alongside the horse's hindquarters. The rider applies the aids for piaffe, and the assistant, if necessary, taps with the whip to encourage the horse to flex his hind legs and to place them further under his body. As soon as the horse steps correctly with diagonal pairs, the forelegs rising higher than the hind legs, he can be asked to carry out this work more energetically. To achieve this the collection has to be built up so that just before asking for piaffe-like steps, walk pirouettes and transitions from a shortened trot to halt (and vice versa) can be performed.

It is advisable to teach piaffe first, but if the horse is naturally short of impulsion, the passage may be taught before the piaffe, not only to improve the impulsion but to teach the horse to spring energetically off the ground.

Passage

This is a very collected, very elevated and very cadenced trot. Each diagonal pair of feet is raised higher and with a longer period of suspension than for any other trot.

Aims

- The toe of the raised foreleg should be level with the middle of the cannon bone of the other foreleg. The toe of the raised hind leg should be slightly above the fetlock joint of the other hind leg, i.e. as in piaffe.
- The neck should be raised and arched, with the poll as the highest point and the head close to the perpendicular. The horse should remain on the bit, accepting a light contact.
- The hindquarters should be well engaged and the flexion of the knees and hocks should be accentuated, but with graceful elasticity of movement.
- The impulsion should be lively and pronounced and the horse should be able to go smoothly from the passage to the piaffe, and vice versa, without apparent effort and without altering the rhythm.
- The steps should be regular and neither the forehand nor the hindquarters should swing from one side to the other.

Passage. Maximum collection and engagement, with the horse moving forward in a very cadenced, elevated trot.

Execution

The passage is taught usually from the saddle. It is developed out of the piaffe, the collected trot, or sometimes the walk, depending on the abilities and temperament of the horse. It is most usual to teach from the piaffe, as long as the horse has mastered this movement.

The horse is ready to be taught passage when he is capable of positive collection and extension, and of containing his impulsion.

An assistant on the ground may be useful, as he can come close to the hindquarters, with a long whip if necessary, and without upsetting the horse can indicate that more impulsion and elevation are required.

The rider applies his legs, the pressures being in the rhythm of the passage, and he sits deep, using the forward driving influence of his seat (page 50). The hands restrain, saying 'no faster', so that the increased impulsion goes upwards to produce passage – the elevated steps gaining little ground. When passage-like steps are achieved they should be maintained just long enough for the horse to understand that this is what is required and then given a reward.

The rider can reduce the pressure of his legs when the horse goes into passage and cease the pressure when he wants the horse to return to trot.

As with piaffe, regularity in all its aspects is of prime importance. Only when this can be achieved and maintained should the trainer strive for greater elevation. The movement should be smooth and flowing, without jerky prop-like landings of the forelegs, or hollowing of the back.

Care must be taken that the long whip, used to stimulate activity by applying it to the hindquarters, is not employed too much or too often, so that its stimulating effect is lost.

Variations of passage

Each horse has his characteristic natural type of trot, which should appear in his piaffe and passage. This is why there is so much variation in the types of passage performed. Ideally, the speed of the rhythm (tempo) remains the same in piaffe and passage.

DRESSAGE COMPETITIONS

Most serious riders aim to compete in dressage competitions and to achieve success the following are important prerequisites:

- To have a relaxed horse at the competitions. This usually entails frequent visits to shows, whether competing or not, especially with high-spirited, temperamental or young horses.
- Careful organisation of the 'riding-in' period, taking into account the character and abilities of the horse and the test to be performed. The work to be included (lungeing, walking around, loosening up, etc.) and the time it will take should be planned beforehand.
- Study of judges' sheets to ascertain the defects which need most attention and then training accordingly.
- Development of 'arena craft' which entails careful study of the test to be performed, accurate execution of it, good use of the arena, and determination to show off the horse at his best.

CHAPTER

TRAINING THE HORSE TO JUMP

Horses are born with varying degrees of jumping ability. The trainer's task is to develop the horse's ability, giving him the confidence to jump many different types of obstacles and to do so when carrying a rider.

THE HORSE'S JUMPING TECHNIQUE

A horse jumping correctly from a balanced, calm, yet energetic approach to an obstacle appears to do so with ease. During the last few strides of the approach he stretches his head and neck forward and downwards, then raises them to spring upwards off his forehand. This takes place a moment before the hind feet meet the ground. The powerful muscles of the hindquarters and thighs, and the leverage of the hips, stifles, hocks and fetlocks, push the horse upwards and forwards over the obstacle.

During take-off and over the obstacle, the horse's back should be rounded, not hollow, with the withers as the highest point and with the head and neck stretched forward to help his balance (known as basculing).

On descent, the head and neck rise slightly and the forelegs meet the ground one after the other, followed by the hind legs.

This style is the most efficient method of jumping and demands least effort from the horse. But it takes time to build up the muscles and to develop the suppleness to enable him to jump in this way. Rushed training usually results in incorrect muscle development, less efficient styles (e.g. a hollow back in mid-air) and often eventually – because it takes an effort to jump – a loss of confidence and refusal.

The muscles which should be developed through flat work, riding out, especially up and down hills, and gymnastic jumping exercises, are as follows :

- The upper neck muscles, not those on the underside.
- The shoulder and forearm.
- Back and loin, which are probably the most important.
- Second thigh muscles.

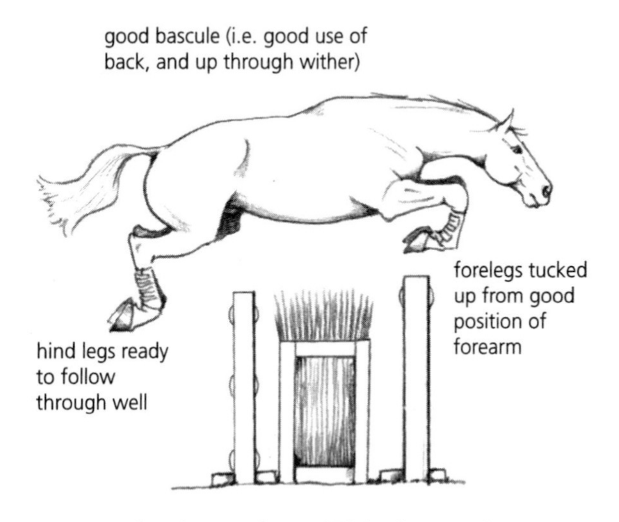

Horse showing good use of his body over a jump.

THE TRAINING PROGRAMME

The work for at least the first year of the horse's ridden life is common to an eventer, a jumper and a dressage horse. He should be backed as described in Chapter 8, and trained on in the way described in Chapter 11, the Preparatory Stage.

The flat work is vital in order to develop the correct muscles and the controlled riding necessary to jump in the above style. In the case of the potential show jumper, greater emphasis can be placed on jumping in conjunction with this flat work. Easy obstacles should be used so that he gradually builds up his ability and confidence.

When he is being backed, and during the early riding days, he can be lunged over trotting poles and very small fences. If the facilities are available he could be loose-schooled. After he relaxes when ridden, and when he is sufficiently obedient and fit, the rider can take him over trotting poles, then progress gradually to small obstacles, with the size and variety of the jumps being slowly increased.

The rate of progress will depend upon the ability of the horse and rider, but the essential factors are:

- The jumping should be fun for the horse, so he must not be asked too much for his stage of training, nor should he be asked to jump when tired. Schooling sessions over jumps should be short.
- Slightly more difficult fences may be tackled when the horse can jump the easier obstacles in the styles described above, but if at any time he loses his confidence, return to the easier obstacles. It is important that in each jumping lesson he is loosened up over trotting poles and/or small fences; gradually progressing to larger obstacles.

Lungeing over small obstacles

The horse first learns to jump without a rider on his back, on the lunge. Start by walking over a pole on the ground, progress to trotting over a series of poles and to jumping solid single obstacles. Remember at all times that it is difficult for the horse to jump off a turn and it takes great skill and experience on the part of the lunger to give him the necessary assistance. Therefore, for most trainers it is advisable to restrict the work on the lunge to trotting poles and single obstacles of not more than about 1m (3ft). For techniques of lungeing over obstacles see pages 81–82.

Loose schooling over obstacles

If the horse can be encouraged to jump loose, calmly, rhythmically and with impulsion, he will learn to look after himself and to develop a good style of jumping. Damage can be done with inadequate facilities, and/or inexperienced trainers, resulting in the horse running out, refusing, or starting to rush his fences. Like lungeing, loose schooling is only of value if done well.

Requirements

- An indoor school or small enclosure from which it is impossible for the horse to escape, or a jumping lane consisting of a series of small fences.
- If an indoor school or enclosure is used, the obstacles should have wings to discourage the horse from running out.
- The horse should be obedient to aids of the voice and the lunge whip.

Techniques

The horse, wearing a headcollar or cavesson and protective boots, should be led around the school once or twice and then let loose and sent round at the trot, driven on when necessary by his trainer's voice and lunge whip. An assistant is needed and should be responsible for driving the horse forward in one half of the school. The trainer and assistant should never be in front of the horse as he moves round the track.

When the horse trots calmly and willingly around the school, an obstacle with wings can be erected. It is advisable to place the poles on the ground, and only when the horse trots over them confidently should they be raised. The best position for the obstacle is usually soon after the corner. Placing poles (see page 125), of 2.4–2.9m (8–9ft), or 5.5–6m (17½–20ft) in front of the jumps are advisable to stop the horse rushing, or arriving at an awkward take-off position. Alternatively, a pole can be placed diagonally in the corner and the small obstacle 16m (52ft) away from it.

It is vital for the trainer and the assistant to present the horse straight at the fence and not to chase him into it. It is essential for the horse to jump of his own accord, encouraged by the voice and the presence of the whip. Obstacles should never be 'trappy', nor too high. At a later stage multiple fences may be used.

The horse should be rewarded frequently during loose-schooling sessions. After a few good circuits he should be stopped, patted, and occasionally given titbits.

Jumping with a rider

The horse should be ready to jump with a rider only after he has learned to jump without a rider, has been backed, is fit and responsive to the aids.

General principles

- It is advisable when jumping to have an assistant present to put up obstacles, to ensure that the distances between fences are correct, and also for reasons of safety.
- The obstacles should be solid or substantial so that the horse does not become careless through finding it easy to hit fences. At the same time, they should be 'inviting', to encourage him to jump and not to run out, and should be kept small enough to prevent him being over-faced.
- Distances between the obstacles and the placing and trotting poles should be 'correct' until an advanced stage of training.
- The young horse should be started over fences with which he is familiar and which he has jumped successfully on the lunge. When trying a 'strange' obstacle it is advisable to make it small in height; to show it to him first; to let him sniff at it; and with nervous horses, to follow an experienced horse over the fence. At all costs, refusals should be avoided.
- Jumping can cause strain on a young horse's tendons and feet. Sprains and lameness can result, particularly if the ground is too hard or too soft, or if the horse is not fit enough for the work demanded. Long jumping sessions should be avoided.

NB There is no need to jump massive fences at home. The aim of the trainer is to familiarise the horse with all types of obstacles and to develop a style which will make jumping as easy as possible. This can be achieved over low obstacles, and even advanced horses need not practise over more than 1.2m (4ft) obstacles.

Method of riding

The rider must be a competent horseman if he is to do this work without hindering his horse. Although remaining in control he should not try to 'place' the horse (adjusting his stride so that he takes off in a particular position).

After presenting his horse straight at the obstacle he should have the following aims in mind:

- To sit as still as possible in the correct position.
- To retain a light rein contact.
- Although allowing the horse as far as possible to approach and jump the obstacles in his own way, sufficient impulsion is essential and at times the rider might have to generate this with his legs and – if necessary – with his seat and taps of the whip. (See pages 85–86.)
- The horse will find it easier to jump in the correct style if he approaches the fence in balance, and therefore with rhythm. Thus the rider should help his horse to establish a rhythm and should not rush or shorten up into a fence.

In the early stages of jump training, the horse should be fitted with a neckstrap or a breast plate – which on occasion even the most experienced rider may need to hold (or the mane) if he is to avoid interfering with the horse's mouth.

The correct position for the rider is described in Chapter 4. It is usual with a young horse to adopt the forward seat, out of the saddle, in order to give the horse's back the freedom to work. However, the seat aids can be used momentarily with a horse who tries to stop, or who lacks impulsion. When working over trotting poles it is vital for the horse's back to be able to move freely and not to be made rigid or hollow. It is usual, therefore, to adopt rising trot; although sitting trot in a forward seat is acceptable for a rider with a good seat and a horse who is strong and supple in his back.

The stages of training

Trotting poles

Work over poles on the ground, at first singly and then in series, is an essential part of a young horse's general education. It is a useful gymnastic exercise which teaches him to lower his head and neck, to round his back, to flex his joints and also to coordinate the action of his limbs.

Distances between poles

Whether on the ground or raised, these must accommodate the horse's stride exactly. For most horses and ponies, except very small ones, the optimum distances are 1m (3ft 3in.) for the walking and 1.3–1.4m (4ft 3in.–4ft 6in.) for trotting. The latter is based on the trotting stride of the average horse. Uncoordinated or big horses need 1.5m (5ft); ponies may need 1.2m (4ft). It is vital to maintain correct distances between poles on the ground. Slight adjustments should be made to suit the strides of different horses and the going (heavy going needs shorter; firm going needs longer). An assistant on the ground should be ready to re-position displaced poles or to adjust distances when they do not suit the stride of the horse.

To raise the poles

These are best put on blocks which have been slightly hollowed out to enable the pole to be fitted and not to roll when hit. Light plastic blocks are ideal.

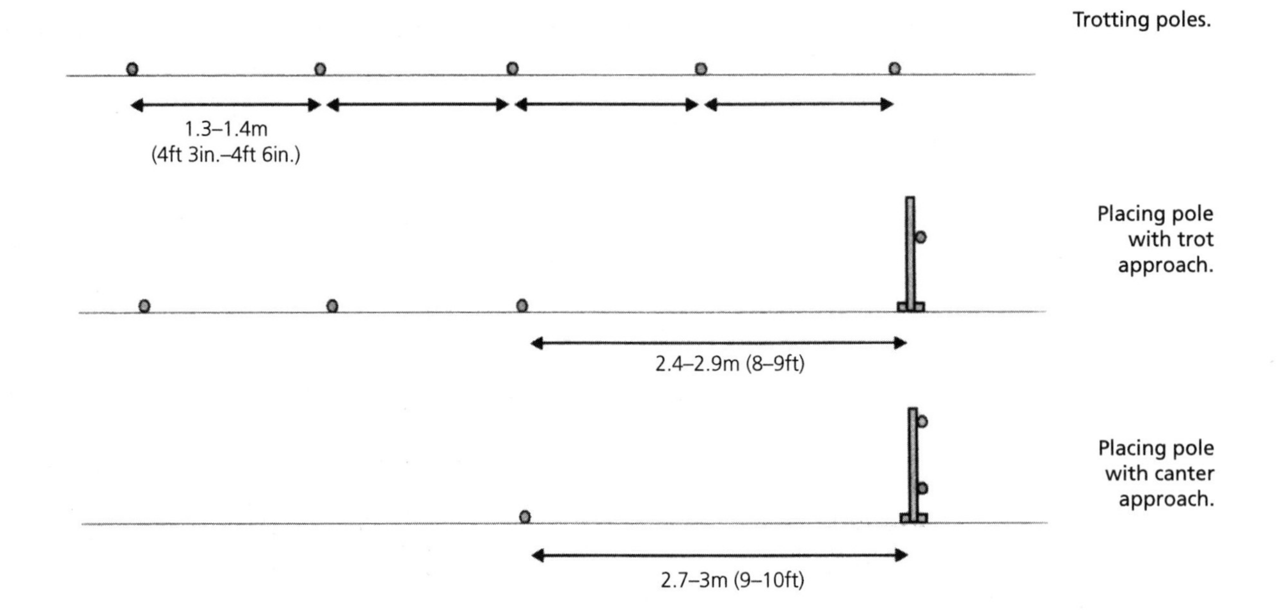

Trotting poles.

Placing pole with trot approach.

Placing pole with canter approach.

Technique

First walk the horse over a single pole. When he does this calmly, the number can be increased to two, three and then four. The poles can then be altered to trotting distances. It is important for the horse to remain calm and to maintain a rhythm. If he gets excited, it sometimes helps to remove alternate poles. He can be trotted in a circle until he settles, and when he does so the poles can be tried again.

Introducing obstacles

When the horse trots over the poles correctly and calmly, a very small obstacle can be erected beyond the last trotting pole. It should look inviting, should not exceed 38cm (1ft 3in.) in height, and preferably should consist of cross-bars which direct the horse towards the centre of the fence. The aim is for the horse to land over the last pole and, without taking a stride, take off over the obstacle. The average horse needs between 2.6m (8ft) and 2.9m (9ft) in front of the fence. Distances should be adjusted for long- or short-striding horses.

Placing poles

In order to help the horse arrive at a good position for take-off, especially in the early stages, when the rider should not interfere, it is advisable to use either trotting poles as above, or a single placing pole, which should be 2.6–2.9m (8–9ft) in front of the jump.

Types of obstacle

As soon as the horse can jump a particular fence at the end of a line of trotting poles, or after a placing pole, calmly and in good style, he can be asked to jump a slightly higher, wider, or different type of obstacle in the same manner.

Single fences

The horse must gradually be introduced to fences (which have groundlines) without trotting poles or a placing pole. The horse should learn to think for himself and should adjust his stride. If a horse starts to rush the fence with inexperienced riders (and for the first few jumps in any lesson) reversion to use of a placing pole is of value.

Combinations

The horse must gradually be introduced to series of fences between which he can take one or two strides. These should start very low so that the horse can gain his confidence.

A placing pole is usually introduced at the beginning of a series of fences to help the horse meet the first jump correctly.

A placing pole is usually advisable in front of a small upright, then another fence at one stride (3.6m/18ft) to a second fence at two strides (8.2m/27ft).

As the horse becomes more confident and proficient, extra fences can be added and the heights and distances altered. The aim is to have the horse jumping in good style with a clear take-off platform.

This means:

- His front legs and hind legs should take off from almost the same place.
- He should bend his front legs upwards, not backward, and they should remain a pair.
- He should jump straight and not twist in the air.
- He should jump calmly and in a good rhythm.

The distances between fences which suit most horses are in multiples of 2.7m (9ft) to 3.3m (11ft) with the fences not over 1m (3ft 3in.). If the horse bends his front legs backwards, the distances are too short; if he flattens in outline between the fences, the distances are too long. The first fence should always be the smallest with the last fence the largest.

By altering the distances the horse can be taught to shorten and lengthen his stride and thus become more athletic. It is important to alter both heights and distances very gradually so that he does not lose confidence.

Cantering

The non-jumping strides at the above distances are taken at the canter, but the initial approach should be at the trot. In the early stages of jump training it is advisable to approach all the fences at the trot as at this gait the horse is usually more balanced and the slower speed encourages him to bascule. However, some trainers work exclusively in canter from the start of a horse's training. Some riders allow their horses to break into canter just before the obstacle, but it is not advisable to make the entire approach at canter until the horse's work on the flat at this pace is satisfactory, and the fences are higher than about 1m (3ft 3in.). At the canter the horse takes tiny obstacles in his stride naturally, but this does not develop his bascule and will encourage a rather flat jump.

Changing the distances

When the horse jumps combinations and grids with correct distances, calmly and in a fluent style, then the distances can be varied, but by inches only at a time, to teach him to jump from both long and short strides. It is best to keep any series of fences either for short strides or for long. Altering short and long distances is very difficult and is inadvisable for all except top horses and riders.

Varying the fences

The horse must be taught to jump all types of fences with confidence. He should be introduced to miniature versions of all the fences found in the show ring – brightly coloured obstacles, walls, triple bars, oxers, planks, brushes, barrels, etc. When riding out, every opportunity can be taken to jump the young horse over unfamiliar obstacles, such as ditches, banks, hedges, logs, etc., as long as they are low enough not to over-face the pupil.

Tackling water jumps should also come into the training programme. Firstly, the horse must learn not to be frightened of water, so he can be walked through puddles and made to jump small streams and ditches, preferably following a more experienced horse. He must have encountered a water tray under a fence and learnt to jump with confidence. A water tray can vary in width from 0.9m (3ft) to much wider and is a common sight in many show-jumping classes. The first water jump he is asked to attempt should not be wide (a maximum of 3m/10ft). It is also advisable to put a pole of about 0.9m (3ft) high over the centre of the water to encourage him to jump into the air, not just to pop over the brush into the water.

The rider should try to get the horse to approach the water with a little more speed than for a normal fence and to ask him to take off as close as possible to the water.

Courses

A horse which is to compete must learn to jump series of fences other than in straight lines. Therefore, a short course of fences similar to, but fewer in number and smaller in height than those in the show ring can be erected. The rider should try to give the horse the best possible approach to the fence so:

(a) He must not cut the corners but give the horse as many straight strides before the fence as possible.

(b) He must keep the horse balanced and in a rhythm. To do this he will probably need to half-halt and collect his horse immediately on landing over each fence and to make a great effort to turn each corner correctly.

(c) The horse must have enough impulsion (see pages 85–86) to tackle the fences, but impulsion must not be confused with speed. Going fast will tend to make the horse flatten over the fences.

Jumping at speed

Most jump-offs are against the clock, so any horse and rider having had sufficient training to make winning a possibility must learn how to jump a course at speed. Galloping into the fences is rarely advisable with young horses, who tend to flatten and become careless. The horse must learn to jump fences at angles and to be balanced enough to cut a corner and – having taken one or two strides – to jump the obstacle.

The rider should aim to maintain impulsion and rhythm when practising these techniques over small obstacles.

SOLVING JUMPING PROBLEMS

Refusing

This is a problem which the trainer should try to avoid at all costs. Therefore never ask a horse to jump a fence at a height which he and his rider are not capable of negotiating. With strange obstacles, give the horse every opportunity to gain his confidence by starting very low, by having a more experienced horse jump first, and by making the fence as inviting as possible with a ground line, good width and wings to stop run-outs.

Should the horse refuse: if it is through lack of confidence or poor riding, lower the fence before trying again. If the horse is doing it out of mischief and is starting to do it frequently, he should be reprimanded once, and ridden strongly into fences.

If a horse that normally jumps well starts refusing, it is probable that he is in pain. Steps must be taken to discover the reason. It may be his feet, his back or his mouth that is hurting him.

Rushing into the fence

This makes it difficult for the horse to be balanced and to arrive at the correct take-off position. It is often considered to be due to over-eagerness: but, on the contrary, it is usually due to lack of confidence and the horse trying to get the frightening operation (of jumping) over as quickly as possible.

To correct

- The rider must give the horse confidence, which is best done by jumping frequently over small single fences, so that it becomes part of the routine rather than a major operation. Consecutive fences should not be attempted. After jumping a fence, settle the horse before attempting another.
- The rider can circle his horse in front of the fence until he settles into a rhythm, and only then allow him to jump.
- Trotting poles can be placed in front of the obstacle. It is usually best to walk into the first pole of the line.
- Small grids can be used frequently.
- Jump on a circle with a short approach.

Rushing after the fence

It is important for the horse to be balanced as soon as possible after the fence and not to rush off. If the voice and half-halts (but not pulling on the reins) are not effective then place a pole at either 6.5m (21ft) or 9.5m (31ft) after the fence.

Taking off too close

Horses which take off too close to a fence lack scope and/or confidence.

To correct

- The horse must be given sufficient impulsion to clear the fence.
- A take-off rail should be placed about a foot out from the base of each fence.
- The distances between combination fences can be gradually lengthened so that he learns to extend his stride and to take off further away.
- Use placing poles to get the horse to stand back.

Jumping with a hollow back

Horses tend to jump with a flat or hollow back if they approach the fences too fast and/or take off far away.

To correct

- Jump fences out of a trot rather than a canter.
- Use placing poles in front of the fences to encourage him to get closer to the fences. Begin with a distance which is easy for him, and gradually shorten it so that he has to take off closer to the fence.
- Jump plenty of low, wide parallels which encourage a horse to bascule and to fold his forelegs.
- Use plenty of grids with relatively short distances between the fences.

Familiarisation

A horse's first show is usually a nerve-racking experience. It is therefore advisable to take him to a show before he starts competing and to get him relaxed in this stimulating atmosphere.

CHAPTER

CROSS-COUNTRY TRAINING

To be successful across country the horse must be able to cope with the great range of problems found in today's competitions. Both horse and rider must learn through careful thorough training and familiarisation how to approach and jump the variety of fences met in eventing.

Early training

The aims of early training are to teach the horse:

- To regulate pace and cope with slopes and all types of going, including entering water.
- To respect solid fences.
- To become a safe conveyance across country by being encouraged from the beginning to work things out for himself.
- To be tough and able to perform in all types of weather. He should not be over 'cosseted'.

Flat work

This should continue in the manner described in Chapters 11 and 12.

Jumping exercises

The horse's athletic ability is built up over a period of months by varying the exercises over trotting poles, grids and small fences, jumped at angles from both trot and canter. At these angled fences the rider must be able to use each hand independently to guide the horse effectively and keep the legs against the horse's sides at all times.

Jumping exercises should be carried out up to two to three times a week in between flat work and hacks, and these should be based on the work discussed in the previous chapter.

Hacking

Whilst out hacking the horse should learn to cope with all types of going and terrain. He has to be able to balance himself when riding up and down hills and over rough ground. It is best to use a loose rein as much as possible so that he can think and hold himself without reliance on the rider.

Popping over little fences, such as logs and ditches, when out hacking will teach him to be alert and quick-thinking. Water should be ridden through and over whenever possible.

It is vital that the horse is never frightened, so:

- Everything attempted should be within the horse's capabilities for his stage of training.
- The fences should be safe, with good take-offs and landings. A nasty experience in the early stages could undermine a horse's confidence.

Schooling over cross-country fences

This can begin once the horse is (a) confident when jumping fences on flat ground or just over 1m (3ft 3in.), (b) balanced and controllable enough to jump combinations, and (c) able to lengthen and shorten his stride. Several sessions may be required. The first should be over straightforward fences of different types up to 0.9m (3ft). In succeeding sessions, start with a few simple obstacles and gradually increase the questions asked by including ditches and rails, steps, banks, bullfinches, rails at varying angles, and corners. The horse should be progressively familiarised with the types of fence which are met with on cross-country courses. Always finish on a good note – before the horse becomes too tired.

Hunting

Some horses learn the techniques of cross-country jumping much more quickly than others, but they all benefit from a season's hunting, which teaches both rider and horse to go boldly across country and to think quickly over unfamiliar ground. This is how horses learn to produce a 'fifth leg' and become adept at jumping the unexpected.

Hunter trials

Once the horse can jump small cross-country fences confidently, he can be entered in novice hunter trials.

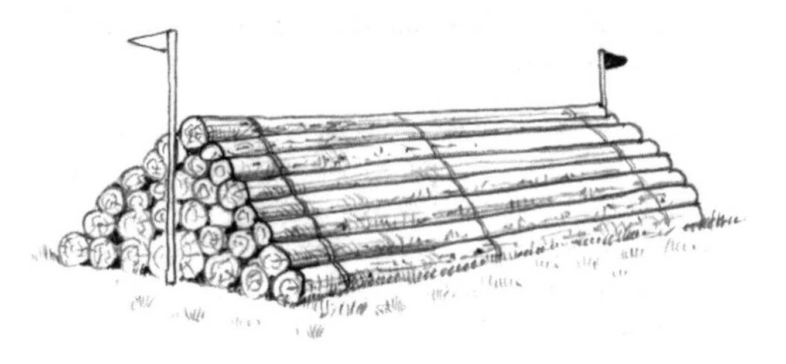

Log pile – a useful obstacle which can be jumped from either direction.

Pair classes may benefit the timid horse if a more experienced horse is the pair and leads to give him confidence.

Progression to more advanced competitions depends on how the horse tackles the small ones. As long as he goes well at the lower level, he can be asked a bit more and the difficulty can be increased as and when the horse is confident enough to cope. Never ever ask too much at once.

TYPES OF FENCE

Cross-country fences can be divided into several categories according to the method of riding needed to negotiate them safely at the faster speed used when cross-country riding.

Respect is needed for every fence. Each type of fence must be treated with respect. All too often it is the simple ones which cause the most trouble. This is usually because most thought goes into approaching and riding the more difficult fences – so that they often cause comparatively few problems. The rider must treat each fence as if it is the most important one, so that the horse is given the maximum help throughout. Ridden in this way, horses build up confidence in their rider and vice versa, and the combination then becomes a partnership, each confident in their ability to jump any course attempted. Confidence is one of the most important aspects of cross-country riding.

Upright fences

Uprights should present few problems, although the degree of difficulty will depend on how and where they are built. The rider must check:

- To see if there is a false groundline (the pole on or nearest to the ground is behind the higher poles). Horse and rider usually judge the take-off point by looking at this lowest pole. If they do so when it is a false groundline they will get too close to the fence.
- If the ground is uneven.

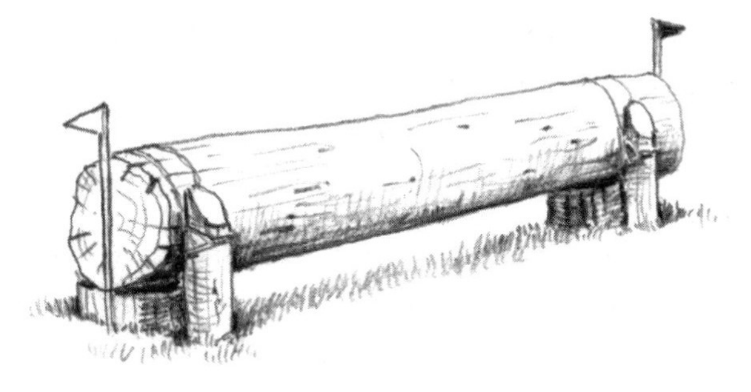

Hanging log.

Bench, or seat, fence.

- Whether the fence can be easily seen from the line of approach.
- The height of the fence.

Aims when riding

- To ride straight at the fence in almost all cases.
- To be accurate, never asking for too much of a stand-off, nor getting too close.
- To build up plenty of impulsion if the upright is sited on the top of a hill. This will ensure that the horse's hocks are underneath him before he takes off.
- If at the bottom of a hill, uprights must be approached at a steady pace, making sure that the horse is not on his forehand but well between the hand and leg. Then he can take off easily yet remain balanced on landing.

Spread fences

Aims when riding

- To ride with plenty of impulsion. Approaching too slowly will necessitate last minute effort, which could easily frighten a young horse.
- To take care not to let the horse stand off too far and so make the fence unnecessarily wide.
- If the spreads are sloped, the rider should not ask for too big a stand-off and should allow the horse as much rein as he needs.
- If they are parallels they should be ridden-at straight and accurately, keeping the horse well between hand and leg, and not on the forehand. If he is to avoid disastrous results he must get off the ground in time to clear the front rail.

Ditches and open water

- Ditches must be ridden at strongly, with energy but not too much speed, particularly on the 'spooky' type of horse who may tend to have a last-minute look but will then still go due to the impulsion created by the rider.
- Open water must be ridden at strongly, but accurately, encouraging the horse to spring up into the air. Strong legs are applied and a good contact on the reins maintained to keep him up so that he jumps the obstacles clearly. Often the edges to ditches and open water are a bit soft.
- Large, wide ditches need very strong riding, creating power with the legs and sometimes with the seat, and a good firm contact on the reins, to encourage the horse to go upwards and forwards. When ridden this way they rarely cause trouble despite their horrific appearance.
- Open ditches with brush and with rails must always be boldly ridden.

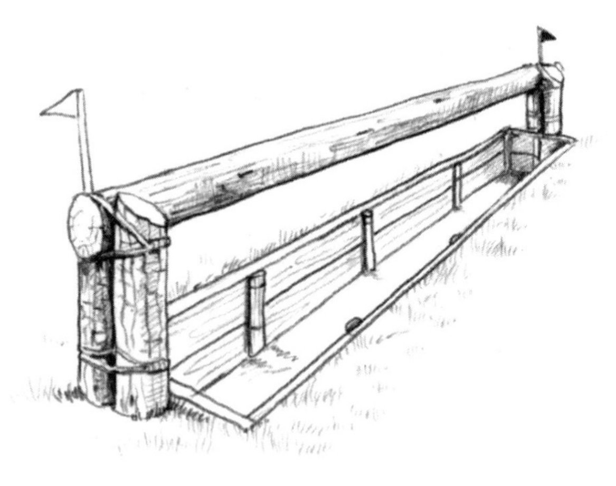

Trakehner.

- Rails over ditches, trakehners (see drawing above) and tiger traps often cause trouble because the horse (and rider) tend to look down into them and then lose the impulsion to clear the fence. Firm riding with plenty of leg, encouraging the horse forward and upward, is needed at this type of fence which, although simple, often causes problems on novice courses.
- Angled rails over a ditch are generally best approached straight and in the middle, or slightly to the side, where the rail is farthest away, as the ditch can help by acting as a nice ground-line.

Water

Water must be ridden into with a great deal of thought and care.

Assessing a water jump

It is difficult to judge the pace at which any fence into water is best jumped unless the depth and landing are known. Therefore, before attempting it on horseback, it is advisable to walk through the water to ensure that the base is even and does not have any holes or soft patches, to measure the depth, and to find out whether the water is fast flowing or still.

Aims when riding

- The approach should not be too fast, as the drag of the water on landing tends to tip the horse on to his forehand. Coming in too slowly, however, can cause an unnecessary stop. A good, strong trot or 'bouncy canter' is usually the best pace.
- The horse should be encouraged to jump out as far as possible so that he does not land too steeply.
- As most water jumps involve some degree of drop, the rider adjusts his position to prevent being thrown forward on landing. This helps the horse keep his balance and enables him to be ridden forward immediately.
- Fences in water or which have water in front of them are best approached at a trot to avoid sending up too much spray, which can unsight the horse.

Many falls would be prevented if water were ridden at a sensible pace. A definite, controlled approach and control on landing are the two vital factors.

Combinations

All combinations require accurate and controlled riding and the more difficult ones really test the athletic ability of a horse.

Aims when riding

- **Rails at varying angles to each other**. These need practice at home so that the horse is familiar with all the differing forms of one and two stride distances (page 125). The line of approach is of the utmost importance. Once the best line has been determined, a straight route through the obstacle is the secret of success, Having decided on the route which will give the horse the best distances, it is vital to arrive at the exact spot for take-off. Therefore a line through the obstacle is determined by going from one specific landmark straight towards another, e.g. from a conveniently situated tree to a certain telegraph pole.

- **Bounces**, which demand great agility, are very difficult for stiff horses. They must be approached steadily, but with plenty of impulsion so that the horse resembles a tightly coiled spring being released over each jump. Approaching this type of obstacle too fast with the horse on the forehand is inviting disaster. Controlled forward impulsion should be aimed at. Grid work is the introduction to this, but practice over higher fences with wider distances is necessary to teach the horse to use himself correctly. Start with very small fences with the distance between 3m (l0ft) and 3.3m (11ft). As the height is increased the distance can be lengthened to 3.6m (12ft) or more to suit the strides of the horse.

  Bounces demand great effort from the horse and should not be overdone. Two or three successful attempts are sufficient. The horse should always be well loosened up before practising this type of exercise.

Rails and ditch complexes

These are fences which catch out the unwary and should be mastered before tackling them in competition.

A rails–ditch–rails complex. The rails of the ditch should be fixed, so that if hit by a horse he does not carry them down the bank with him, which could cause a fall.

To practise

Once the horse is confident when jumping all types of ditches he can be introduced to rails one or two strides immediately after a ditch and then progress to jumping rails in front of the ditch. As soon as he is confident he can be asked to jump rails–ditch–rails, varying the distances of the rails on either side of the ditch.

Aims when riding

- The approach is all-important, but the technique depends on the siting of the fence. The usual siting is downhill to the first section with the last element uphill. These fences require steady but determined riding. The horse may not see the ditch until the last moment, so the important factor is for him to have sufficient impulsion and to be ridden forward in the last few strides, which will make it difficult for him to stop.
- As the 'out' rails of these complexes are often uphill and can be rather close to the ditch, the horse must be kept in balance and not allowed to 'launch off' from the bottom and then fail to clear the final element.
- The position of the rider at such fences is particularly important. If he gets too far in front or behind the movement of the horse at the crucial moment he may hinder the horse and prevent him from completing the fence.

Banks

Aims when riding

- Banks must be ridden at with great impulsion, but not too fast, as when jumping uphill a horse loses momentum. This is an important principle of cross-country riding. Momentum is gained when jumping downhill, and is lost uphill. Allowance must be made for this.
- They should be approached straight.
- Once on top of a bank the rider must maintain forward impulsion.
- On landing, balance the horse by maintaining an upright position and not allowing the legs to move backwards.
- With a Normandy bank – a bank with rails off – maintain plenty of forward impulsion, especially at those fences designed for an on-off jump. The horse should be allowed to jump out well to avoid a steep landing, which may follow if this type of jump is ridden at too slowly.

Corners

Corners require an accurate, calculated approach and an ability to ride straight. It is safest to choose the line as shown above right.

Assessing corners

The line of approach must be determined, allowing enough room to jump: not so close to the apex and the flag that there is danger of running out, yet not too far in, where the fence becomes too wide to jump safely. Study the fence carefully on foot, so that the spot to be jumped is clear. Then move back from the fence to see the line that you wish to approach. Choose a suitable landmark which will not be obscured when riding – that is, on the far side – and aim to ride at it to ensure that the fence is met absolutely right.

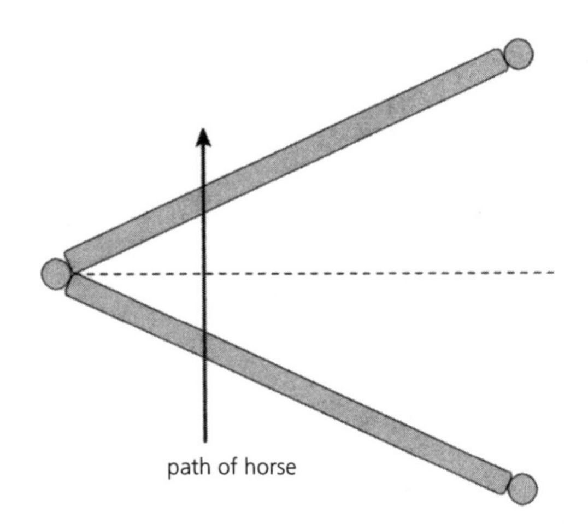

A corner fence showing the safest path for the horse: i.e. at right angles to a line which bisects the corner.

Aims when riding

Ride to the landmarks. Take the fence with precision. This will ensure a good ride over a corner fence.

Steps and drops

Aims when riding

- Steps up require enough impulsion to overcome the shortening effect of jumping uphill. If there are several, the energy must be maintained to the top.
- Drop fences or steps down require the horse to be steadied so that he does not land with too much impetus which he will then be unable to control. The rider should keep the weight upright and off the forehand. Steps down are best approached from trot.

JUMPING AT SPEED

Cross-country jumping requires a faster speed than show jumping. The rider should help the horse to negotiate the solid, fixed obstacles by riding sensibly and keeping the horse under control at all times. As the horse gains experience the speed can be increased, but the horse must always be listening and obedient so that he can be balanced for the turns and fences. A good steady rhythm, avoiding unnecessary pulling, and aiming always for the most direct route between one fence and another, are more important than speed and will take less out of the horse.

The rider's position

He should be in the galloping position with shortened leathers, the seat out of the saddle, and a good contact on the reins (see illustration on page 42). On approaching a fence the horse should be steadied and balanced with the legs. The rider should lower his seat to the degree necessary to maintain the impulsion needed by a particular fence, e.g. steadier at uprights than those with a good groundline. Upon landing, the galloping position should then be resumed.

Galloping

The gallop must be perfected before entering more advanced events. This will also help to clear the horse's wind and make him fit. When out hacking, the horse should learn to canter on strongly, remaining obedient and calm. It should be remembered that flat-out galloping is not required on cross-country courses, and when preparing for one-day events it is important to practise cantering at a strong pace up and down hills and over fences. For two- and three-day events the horse should learn to gallop, but it is a mistake to over-gallop him as this will wear him out or lame him before getting to the competition.

Galloping should always be on the best possible ground and, if possible, slightly uphill, as this puts far less strain on the horse's legs while still helping to clear his wind.

Galloping should not be attempted until the horse is fit and has been in serious work for at least six to eight weeks. Start with a five- or six-furlong gallop, being careful to keep the horse balanced and well between hand and leg. Begin fairly slowly and then push the horse on for the last quarter mile, to make him blow. Bring him back steadily to a walk. Never allow him to flounder along. Loosen the girths and walk until he has cooled off and stopped blowing.

The amount of galloping and distance will depend on each horse and on the terrain, as galloping uphill makes the horse work harder than on the flat.

INTERVAL TRAINING

This is an alternative to galloping as a means of getting a mature eventer fit. Several short periods of work are alternated with brief recovery periods (the intervals). It is based on methods devised by Jack le Goff (the French trainer who so successfully coached the USA's horse trials teams in the 1970s and 1980s) and adapted from interval-training methods used by athletes.

Principles

- The body will adapt itself to the stress of demands made upon it, as long as it is given time. Therefore repeatedly small but increased demands are made upon it.
- The intervals are timed so that the recovery is not quite achieved before the next period of work.
- The work periods are designed to avoid maximum stress, so that the respiratory, cardiovascular and muscular systems are all gradually developed.
- It is used not more than once every three or four days as it takes this long for the metabolism to return to normal.

Use

Interval training is only suitable for

- A mature horse.
- A sound horse.
- A horse who has completed 4 to 8 weeks of basic

fittening and conditioning work (i.e. capable of hacking for one and a half to two hours).

Timing

Six to twelve weeks of interval training are needed before a three-day event.

The programme

A programme is devised so that the distance and speeds are gradually increased. A number of competitions can be integrated into the interval-training programme to prepare for a three-day event.

Before cantering, the horse should be warmed-up with 30 minutes of walking and trotting.

After cantering he should be cooled down by gentle work for up to an hour. This is essential to help the vascular system remove waste products accumulated during exercise.

All work must be carried out with the horse going into the bridle and on the aids.

An individual programme

It is vital for the programme to be adjusted to suit the needs of the individual horse. The aspects which can be varied are:

- The **rest intervals**. Range of one to four minutes. Four minutes may be needed for the horse to 'almost' recover at the beginning of training, but only one minute if the horse is very fit.

Work periods

- **Duration**. Range 3 to 12 minutes, but in total a training session should not be more than 35 minutes. The aim is to work up to cantering at least the distance of the steeplechase and cross-country combined.

  NB Excitable horses can be cantered for longer distances more slowly.

- **Number**. A maximum of three work periods.

- **Frequency**. Interval training may be used once to twice a week. With a young horse, once a week might be sufficient, but it is usual to progress to twice a week (every four days).

- **Speeds**. These range from trot, through canter to a gallop at about 600 metres per minute. Young horses might begin their interval training with trot periods, but the major part of the work is done at 'half speed' – a canter of approximately 400m/min. As the horse becomes fitter it can be increased to 500m/min and eventually for ½ mile or 1 mile periods at 600m/min.

  NB Horses competing in one- or two-day events before the three-day event need not do faster work until the last two or three weeks. Horses with a history of leg problems should work up hills instead of doing the faster work, and depending on their 'wind' may need one or two pipe-openers, going at close to maximum speed for 500m uphill 10 days before the event.

- **Terrain**. If hilly, canter distances can be reduced by up to 25 per cent.

  NB Varied terrain helps to keep the horse fresh.

- **Work on non-cantering days**. If the horse works strongly for 1½ hours on these days, less cantering may be needed. If he does not do much, more may be needed. Work on non-cantering days depends on the particular trainer and is a major cause of differences in cantering programmes.

  NB After a competition a horse will need usually a minimum of seven days before cantering again.

- **The horse**. The type of horse and how recently he has been fit affects the programme. A small Thoroughbred which has been very fit recently needs less work than a cold-blooded horse which has never been really fit.

NOTES ON CANTER WORK FOR THE EVENT HORSE

- On approximately the fourth week of basic fittening, start the basic canter work.
- Canter work can be carried out approximately every four days; this can be varied slightly to fit in with competitions and other training requirements.
- Prior to any canter work, 20 minutes of continual trot work is needed to warm up the horse; this can include some hill work.
- Some horses benefit from increasing hill work in trot and canter, and decreasing the canter times.
- From the sixth canter workout onwards, it is a good idea to do some work at higher speeds to open up the lungs, for 30–45 seconds during the workout.
- A short trot after the final canter is helpful in letting the horse cool down slowly.
- The one-minute rest period can be extended if the heart rate has not returned to the normal resting rate.
- The above are guidelines only.

SAMPLE FITTENING PROGRAMMES

Sample fittening programmes for a horse preparing for a 1* and 2* three-day event are given on pages 139 and 140.

EVALUATING FITNESS

Heart and respiration rates

- Heart rates can vary, but once a norm has been established a record of the levels and recovery rates of the heart and respiration help in the evaluation of fitness. For an accurate comparison the same amount of exercise and the same intervals after work must be taken. One method is to compare rates every 10 days by cantering up the same hill, stopping, and taking the rates after one, five and ten minutes. As training progresses, the rates should drop.
- The pulse at rest is normally between 36 and 44 beats per minute and top rate is over 200. For maximum training effect the pulse rate should stay between 100 and 150 while the horse is working.
- Respiration at rest is normally 10 to 16 and it should not go above 100 during work.
- 'False' readings can occur, as an excited horse has a high pulse and a hot horse can respire very quickly. Establish a normal pattern for each individual horse in a given situation.

Feel

It is the experienced eye of the trainer and the feel of the rider which judge the fitness of the horse and his best programme of work. There is no substitute for knowing one's horse, for he is a unique living animal with his own capabilities, limitations and requirements.

THE START AND FINISH

The start

This is important, as a quick getaway can save valuable seconds. Practise walking into a start box or similar area.

Keeping quite calm, walk in a small circle until the starter begins the count-down at five seconds. Walk into the box and face away from the exit. Quietly turn round so that the horse is ready and does not get upset. The rider should not fight the exuberant horse. He will settle far more quickly if the rider sits quite still and keeps a firm contact on the reins.

The finish

After passing the finish keep hold of the horse's head and bring him gradually back to a walk. Flopping in on a loose rein at speed is foolish, as tired horses easily break down if they stumble.

SAFETY EQUIPMENT

Safety when jumping cross-country cannot be too strongly stressed. For the horse, over-reach boots, brushing boots, surcingle and a breast plate are strongly advised. Studs should be used behind, and in front if the going is slippery. For the rider, a crash hats and body protector are compulsory in eventing and cross-country competitions.

SUMMARY

The need for patience and thoughtful training cannot be over-stressed: they are vital in the education of a young horse. If time is spent in the beginning gradually increasing the ability and confidence of the horse, the outcome should be rewarded by many happy hours riding across country in what is a thrilling and most exciting aspect of equestrian sport.

Conversion Table

1600m = 1 mile approx.	1/2 speed = 400m/min approx.
2400m = 1 1/2 miles approx.	3/4 speed = 600m/min approx.
3200m = 2 miles approx.	max speed = 800m/min approx.

Possible fitness programme for a horse preparing for a 1* (novice) three-day event

Time scale	Canter (every 4th day)	Minutes at 400m/min	Minutes of rest	Minutes at 400m/min
	1	2	1	2
	2	2	1	2
	3	3	1	3
	4	3	1	3
	5	4	1	4
	6	4	1	4
approx 1 month from start of canter work	7	4.5	1	4.5
	8	4.5	1	4.5
	9	5	1	5
	1st novice horse trial	count as a canter workout; assess fitness on how the horse finishes the XC		
	10	5	1	5
	11	5	1	5
	2nd novice horse trial			
	13	5	1	5
approx 2 months from start of canter work	14	5.5	1	5.5
	3rd novice horse trial			
	15	5.5	1	5.5
	16	6	1	6
	4th novice horse trial			
	17	6	1	6
	18	6	1	6
	5th novice horse trial			
	19	6	1	6
approx 3 months from start of canter work	20	6	1	6

Horse now fit enough to compete at a 1* three-day novice

Possible fitness programme for a horse preparing for a 2* (intermediate) three-day event

Time scale	Canter (every 4th day)	Minutes at 400m/min	Minutes of rest	Minutes at 400m/min
	1	2	1	2
	2	2	1	2
	3	3	1	3
	4	3.5	1	3.5
	5	4	1	4
	6	4.5	1	4.5
approx 1 month from start of canter work	7	5	1	5
	8	5.5	1	5.5
	9	6	1	6
	1st intermediate horse trial	count as a canter workout; assess fitness on how the horse finishes the XC		
	10	6	1	6
	11	6.5	1	6.5
	2nd inter horse trial			
	13	6.5	1	6.5
approx 2 months from start of canter work	14	7	1	7
	3rd inter horse trial			
	15	7	1	7
	16	7.5	1	7.5
	4th inter horse trial			
	17	7.5	1	7.5
	18	8	1	8
	5th inter horse trial			
	19	7.5	1	7.5
approx 3 months from start of canter work	20	8	1	8

Horse now fit enough to compete at a 2* three-day novice

APPENDIX

1 THE BRITISH HORSE SOCIETY

WHAT IS THE BRITISH HORSE SOCIETY?

The British Horse Society is a charity to promote the welfare, care and use of the horse and pony; to develop correct training of the horse; to encourage horsemastership and the improvement of horse management and breeding; and to represent all equine interests.

The Society is internationally recognised as the premier equestrian riding, training and examination organisation in the United Kingdom, and operates an Approvals scheme for all types of equestrian establishment. It incorporates over 400 Riding Clubs and works closely with the Pony Club. The Society is also the national governing body for recreational riding and fully supports the independent sporting disciplines within the British Equestrian Federation.

The BHS plays a major role in equine welfare, safety, provision of access to the countryside, and protection of riding and driving Rights of Way. It represents riders to Government and to the EU in Brussels in all matters, especially those concerning taxation, rates, planning and the law.

Membership benefits include £5 million public liability insurance, personal accident insurance, a yearbook, magazines, special facilities and discounts at BHS functions, and access to BHS advice and support.

At the end of the year 2004 the BHS had over 60,000 members. In addition, Affiliated Riding Clubs represented approximately 38,000 members.

By joining the Society you are helping all who ride. For further information and membership details contact:

The British Horse Society
The Deer Park
Stoneleigh
Kenilworth
Warwickshire CV8 2XZ

tel: 01926 707 700 or 08701 202244
fax: 01926 707 800
email: enquiry@bhs.org.uk
website: www.bhs.org.uk

INDEX

Page numbers in *italics* refer to illustrations